T0356986

PRAISE FOR THE INCREDIBLE JOURNEY
OF PLANTS

"Mancuso is a genial narrator, who tells the story of plants' journeys through well-crafted stories that are embellished by the sweetly decorative watercolors of Grisha Fischer. He effortlessly interweaves science with history, philosophy, and humor and introduces fascinating characters, very much including the plants themselves, which take on human, even heroic, traits." —*Wall Street Journal*

"A gripping series of evolutionary history vignettes about plants that have coexisted either in spite of or due to human intervention...a new perspective on that hazy term, 'nature.'" —*Salon*

"An absorbing overview of botanical history and why its understanding is vital to the earth's future." —*Parade*

"Anecdotes enliven Mancuso's quirky little global history, which argues that plants 'are more sensitive than animals.'" —*Nature*

"[An] elegant and charmingly illustrated survey...The topics of human intervention and plant evolution are gracefully intertwined in discussions of coconut trees, date palms, and bristlecone pines...naturalists and the culinary-inclined will cherish this collection of botanical vignettes." —*Publishers Weekly*

"Illuminating and surprisingly lively...[Mancuso] smoothly balances expansive historical exploration with recent scientific research...An authoritative, engaging study of plant life, accessible to younger readers as well as adults." —*Kirkus Reviews*

"A love letter from a botanist to the plants he studies, written in a breezy and poetic style. Reading this book will give you a whole new appreciation for plants and their many remarkable lifestyles and adaptations. You'll never look at a blade of grass or a forest of trees the same way again!"
—Steve Brusatte, University of Edinburgh paleontologist and *New York Times/Sunday Times* bestselling author of *The Rise and Fall of the Dinosaurs*

"This artfully crafted exposition delightfully delves into the lives of plants by presenting the eight pillars on which those lives are built."
—*Newsweek*, Best Books to Read This Spring

"Mancuso writes playfully; as manifestos go, he knows, his is deeply weird... But this is peculiarity with a purpose. The conceit, an impassioned argument from collectivized flora that cites both atmospheric emissions and anthropocenic despair, forces readers to ask elemental questions. Who—and what—deserves moral consideration when the fate of one species is so often the fate of another? Mancuso's plants, in the end, make some very good points." —*The Atlantic*

"A renowned scientist delivers a simple yet urgent call to action on behalf of Earth's multitude of plants... [a] powerful book... Mancuso concludes his elegant and cogent argument with straightforward advice accessible to anyone... Insightful and arresting, this book offers an achievable road map to a more 'radiant future.'"
—*Kirkus Reviews*

"A marvelously inventive spur to imagination. Plants have many lessons to offer us about thriving and resilience, and these are wonderfully elucidated in this deep green journey."
—David George Haskell, author of the Pulitzer Prize finalist *The Forest Unseen* and John Burroughs Medal recipient *The Songs of Trees*

"Stefano Mancuso's *The Nation of Plants* is brilliant and delightful. A perfect little gem of a book."
—Sonia Shah, author of *The Next Great Migration: The Beauty and Terror of Life on the Move*

"A fantastic and necessary read for any plant enthusiast or environmental activist, *The Nation of Plants* is not merely a missive on the perils of climate change. Rather, the book begins from the whimsical perspective of plants, then weaves scientific fact with historical examples in a moving and inspiring call to action. Apart from the initial address, Mancuso's concrete approach is far from fantastical. *The Nation of Plants* is moving and informative, balancing a love for all things botanical with a passion for listening to and considering the needs of our plant brethren."

—Jessica Roux, author of *Floriography: An Illustrated Guide to the Victorian Language of Flowers*

"In his new book, *The Nation of Plants*, Stefano Mancuso expresses his awe for plants by asking a unique question: What if our Constitution were rewritten by plants? What would be the fundamental laws if the Earth were governed by plants rather than people? Mancuso answers this question by masterfully and thoughtfully linking the stories of people, plants, and plant science. A must-read for anyone who is interested in the historical interactions between people and plants."

—Valerie Trouet, author of *Tree Story: The History of the World Written in Rings*

"In this insightful and pithy tract, Stefano Mancuso convincingly argues that the route to fighting climate change and mass extinction, and to living sustainably on this Earth, begins with a floral point of view. This is the constitution we need."

—Zach St. George, author of *The Journeys of Trees: A Story about Forests, People, and the Future*

"*The Nation of Plants* unveils the long-term relationship between plants and people and explores the rights of all living things. It is a call for cooperation in a world facing persistent environmental degradation. It is a call for our mutual survival."

—Lauren E. Oakes, author of *In Search of the Canary Tree*

"In this brief book, Stefano Mancuso offers what may be the most original solution to the troubling age of humans. What if it were plants, rather than humans, who wrote a constitution for Earthly survival? Mancuso's innovative manifesto is a set of principles for living according to the botanical world. He imagines a new political order based not on the survival of the fittest, but rather on life in community, mutual aid, freedom from borders, and sovereignty for all living beings. In this engaging read, the plant philosopher pushes readers to see how much our survival depends on the well-being of the Nation of Plants—and gives us a radical guide to living according to the rules of life's unsung heroes."

—Elizabeth Hennessy, author of *On the Backs of Tortoises: Darwin, the Galapagos, and the Fate of an Evolutionary Eden*

PRAISE FOR PLANTING OUR WORLD

"Insightful essays about the wondrous qualities of plants and humanity's relationship with them...The reflections are as entertaining as they are educational and showcase the overlooked complexity of plant life. Shot through with wisdom and joy, this will captivate readers."

—*Publishers Weekly*

"[Mancuso] expertly combines his accessible style with pertinent scientific data...An eclectic and fascinating collection that will leave readers wanting more from this appealing guide to the world's flora."

—*Kirkus Reviews*

"When does education stop and learning begin? Stefano Mancuso's *Planting Our World* will let you know. With insatiable curiosity, and not without a tincture of humor, he will bring you on a banana slide that ends up with the moon trees of the Apollo 14 mission in 1971. On the way there, you learn the friction coefficient of the banana skin and you will be surprised!"

—Diana Beresford-Kroeger, author of *To Speak for the Trees*

"Are plants more alive than we are? Not a common question, perhaps, but Mancuso would answer yes. From stumps of the living dead, to trees that tell time, to the slipperiness of banana skins, he is a scientist who tells tall tales that also are true."

—William Bryant Logan, author of *Sprout Lands: Tending the Endless Gift of Trees*

PHYTOPOLIS

PHYTOPOLIS
The Living City

STEFANO MANCUSO

Translated from the Italian
by Gregory Conti

OTHER PRESS
New York

Clivers
Goose Grass

1 Flower
2 Fruit
3 Seed

Aparine

Blackwell delin. sculp et Pinx

Originally published in Italian as *Fitopolis, la città vivente* in 2023
by Editori Laterza, Rome.
Copyright © 2023, Gius. Laterza & Figli
English translation copyright © 2025, Gregory Conti

This book was translated thanks to a grant awarded by the Italian Ministry of
Foreign Affairs and International Cooperation.

Title-page art courtesy of the General Research Division, The New York Public
Library. "Uivers, goose grass." New York Public Library Digital Collections.

Production editor: Yvonne E. Cárdenas
Text designer: Patrice Sheridan
This book was set in Chaparral Pro and Copperplate Gothic STD
by Alpha Design & Composition of Pittsfield, NH

10 9 8 7 6 5 4 3 2 1

Library of Congress Cataloging-in-Publication Data
Names: Mancuso, Stefano, author.
Title: Phytopolis : the living city / Stefano Mancuso ; translated from the Italian
   by Gregory Conti.
Other titles: Fitopolis, la città vivente. English
Description: New York : Other Press, 2025. | Includes bibliographical references.
Identifiers: LCCN 2024023334 (print) | LCCN 2024023335 (ebook) |
   ISBN 9781635425246 (hardcover) | ISBN 9781635425253 (ebook)
Subjects: LCSH: Urban ecology (Sociology) | Urban ecology (Biology) |
   Human ecology. | City and town life. | City planning—Environmental aspects.
Classification: LCC HT241 .M35813 2025 (print) | LCC HT241 (ebook) |
   DDC 307.76—dc23/eng/20241209
LC record available at https://lccn.loc.gov/2024023334
LC ebook record available at https://lccn.loc.gov/2024023335

CONTENTS

PROLOGUE

Over the course of just a few decades, humanity has come
up against a revolution in its ancestral habits. Without our
really being aware of it, but step by step, I would say mile
by mile, our species, which until just a short time ago lived
immersed in nature, inhabiting every corner of the Earth,
has reduced its active range to the point of concentrating
most of its members exclusively inside of urban centers.
In just a few generations, we have transformed ourselves
from a species able to live anywhere into beings specialized
in city life. A revolution comparable only to the transition
from hunter-gatherers to farmers that happened 12,000
years ago.

Today, cities, not the entire planet, are the place where
we live. Consequently, the way we have imagined and constructed them, their efficiency, and the effects of their
existence on the rest of the world now extend far beyond
the realm of urban planning and, on the contrary, have an
impact on the lives of all living beings. Life in the city en-
sures our species improved functionality in many different

fields: from energy consumption to transportation, from education to health care, from work and professional opportunities to cultural advancement. Everything works more efficiently in an urban environment. At the same time, the move away from our natural home is the principal cause of many problems of modern life. In order to resolve this apparently irreconcilable conflict between city and nature, the cities of the future, whether constructed *ex novo* or renewed, will have to bring nature back inside our new habitat, transforming cities into *phytopolises* (*phyto*, or plant + *polis*, or city), living cities in which the relationship between plants and animals approaches the relationship that we find in nature: 86.7 percent plants and 0.3 percent animals (humans included). This would involve dedicating a large part of the surface area of a city to plants, which is the exact opposite of what happens today. I can't think of anything more important than this for the future of humanity: recalibrating our relationships with the other living beings, first among them our relationship with plants.

The relationship between people and plants is a challenging one; it involves something whose very essence escapes the understanding of most of us, despite being so simple it can be described with just one word: *dependence*. Animal life depends on vegetable life. Without plants the life of the entire animal kingdom would be impossible. Plants, in the admirable definition of Kliment Timiryazev, a Russian botanist working at the beginning of the twentieth century, are the link between the Earth and the sun.

Thanks to photosynthesis, plants can perform the apparently miraculous feat of transforming the luminous energy of the sun into the chemical energy (sugars) that allows animals to live and multiply. Photosynthesis is the true engine of life: Water, light, and carbon dioxide combine to produce sugars and oxygen. There is nothing of greater importance; we depend on plants for everything. It is common knowledge that plants are the base of the food chain and that the oxygen that we breathe comes from them. Often, however, it escapes us that fossil fuels (like oil and coal) are composed of the fossils of plants, and that most of the active ingredients in medicines, textile fibers, and building material (wood) is of vegetable origin.

And if all of this still were not enough, add to it that plants are also our home. Literally. Our ancestors were arboreal beings, that is, they lived in trees, as most of the primates who are our closest relatives still do today. This long familiarity with the crowns of trees, with their limbs and foliage, has had more profound effects than we are able to imagine. In a certain sense, our bodies, from their overall structure to the features that we hold to be most characteristically human, faithfully reflect our arboreal genesis. Our binocular vision with eyes pointed forward; the differentiation between our anterior limbs constituted of arms and hands suitable for grasping, and posterior limbs formed by legs and feet suitable for locomotion; our erect posture; our fingers clad with nails instead of claws; the crests on our fingertips that we know as fingerprints, among other things, are all evolutionary modifications that originated to allow primates to live in trees and that have had fundamental consequences for our history.

If you have ever responded to the atavistic impulse to climb a tree, you know that the crown of the tree is a space that is difficult to move around in; a tangle of branches and twigs that grow thinner and thinner toward the perimeter of the crown, where we find the productive part of the tree. In these conditions, having binocular vision makes it easier to judge distances and to move with greater surety; an erect body with prehensile arms is able to climb the trunk and swing among its branches; and, finally, having hands endowed with soft padded fingertips covered with prints and protected by nails makes it possible to reach even the thinnest branches to gather fruit and leaves. Those same hands, suitable for living in trees, also allowed humankind to develop the capacity to make tools.

Much of what makes us human derives from trees. Not only because for millions of years our ancestors lived among their crowns, modeling their own bodies in response to this green environment, but also because, thanks to wood, they succeeded in building their own primary shelters and tools. Humans have coevolved with plants and have always lived in environments in which plants accounted for practically the entire ecosystem. In evolutionary terms, the breaking of this bond is extremely recent. For a few decades now, we have been spending our time in front of computer screens and for three to four generations we have lived inside rooms illuminated with electric light, but before that we were farmers for about five hundred generations, and for something like twenty thousand generations we were hunter-gatherers intimately connected with the natural world and, therefore, with plants, of which that world is almost entirely composed.

Well, twenty thousand human generations do not go by in vain. Those twenty thousand generations of living among plants have a much greater influence on our way of being human than the five hundred generations of agriculture and civilization. Green, for example, is the color of which our species can distinguish the greatest number of different shades. That our eyes are so capable of distinguishing the color of plants, with greater detail than any other color, almost seems a suggestion, as though the very roots of our history indicated where it is important for us to focus our attention. It is as true today as it was three hundred thousand years ago that our capacity to survive depends on plants. However, despite our historical relationship with plants, we now seem intent on imagining ourselves as a species situated outside of and, obviously, above nature. We have erased plants from our horizon, becoming blind to the very world on which we depend.

Put another way, our relationship with plants is not limited simply to our nutritional or energy dependence, however we want to define that, but goes much deeper and involves the strong impact of plants on all aspects of our lives. Even when it comes to constructing or changing how we conceive of our cities, listening to those twenty thousand generations that preceded us and whose home was a forest may turn out to be fundamental. In a period of such drastic changes, in which resilience and the capacity to adapt become fundamental values, imagining our cities as diffuse organisms in community with all other living beings—in short, imagining our *phytopolises* as though they were organized like plants—could bring enormous advantages to our species and to our planet.

One

MAN IS THE MEASURE OF ALL THINGS

"Man is the measure of all things, of those that are, that they are; and of those that are not, that they are not." I'm sure you have heard that before. What exactly Protagoras meant to say with this sentence has long been a matter of debate. Almost certainly, by "man" he did not mean humanity as a whole; instead, he was referring to the individual person: Each person is the measure of what they perceive through their senses, in that, what appears to their senses is true for them. But today we interpret it very freely, and with "man is the measure of all things" we generally refer to the idea that human beings are the only standard for measuring reality.

You're probably asking yourself what Protagoras has to do with a book that is supposed to be about treating cities as plants. The answer is simple: It seems to me to be a good starting point from which to recount how the concept of the human being as the measure of all things—though it has no biological or scientific basis—has become so widespread and has had such importance for our species that it has shaped every aspect of our civilization. In a certain sense, what is most striking about this idea is that, despite its being based on totally erroneous premises, our being convinced of it has shaped the reality that surrounds us. We have made everything, from our societies to our organizations, even our cities, by taking our inspiration exclusively from the way in which we ourselves—the measure of all things—are contrived. Furthermore, by acting on this impulse to make everything in our own image and likeness, we have neglected to observe the functioning of the innumerable, often much more efficacious, robust, and creative other organisms that evolution has produced and experimented with for hundreds of millions of years.

Where does this limitation come from? Why are we not capable of appreciating the innumerable organizational possibilities offered by the life-forms that are different from humankind? In part, I believe it stems from our incurable aversion to everything that is not in conformity with us; every deviation from what we perceive as familiar is felt to be a decline or a deterioration, or even a danger. Tendentially, we proceed according to a binary scheme, simple and economical, because having to choose among many solutions, often only slightly different from one another, is something that does not appeal to our brains. Contrary to what we might think, having too many choices is something that animals, including humans, do not appreciate.

Think about when you're at the supermarket and have to choose between a myriad of similar products displayed on the shelves. Usually, we start from the presumption that the greater the choice, the better the odds of finding a solution that is closest to what we are looking for. After all, that is why businesses, of whatever nature, tend to propose an enormous variety of products often distinguished by imperceptible details. Whether it's clothing, coffee, food, or whatever category of product, the rationale is: From me you can get *exactly* what you're looking for. However, what actually happens is very different and is known as the *paradox of choice*. In 2000, two professors from Columbia and Stanford universities published a study of customers in a California supermarket.[1] They had set up a table of samples of Wilkin & Sons marmalades, and every few hours they changed the offer between a selection of twenty-four marmalades and a limited selection of only six. On average, customers tasted only two marmalades, regardless of the size of the assortment. Thus, the authors of the study discovered that even though the large table with twenty-four marmalades generated more interest (attracted more people who stayed for more time), only 3 percent of the customers that tasted them ended up buying a jar, while the percentage rose to 30 percent in the case of the smaller table with fewer marmalades to choose from. Too much choice tends to create a reaction contrary to what would seem to be logical.

I'm sure that many of you have experienced this sort of inhibition in the face of an excessive number of alternatives. I remember that, as a child, when given the chance to buy just one comic book from an overstocked newsstand,

I would stand there for hours weighing the hypothetical pros and cons of each of them. What paralyzed me was the thought that whatever comic book I chose, another option might be better. I got to the point of preferring, rather than the big newsstands, those little country stores that sold everything (including comic books) and where the choice was limited, to my great relief, to two or three comic books that in other, richer occasions I would never have bought. It's the same phenomenon by which, when it comes time to order in a restaurant, if I can—I don't know about you—I wait for someone else to make the effort to choose and then I ask for the same thing. Still today, I am unable to choose among the many proposed dishes; if it were up to me, restaurants would offer only limited menus. That would make them more efficient and me less anxious.

In essence, our brains do not have a sufficient capacity for calculation to determine the contribution of each of the numerous parameters that need to be pondered in order to make a wise choice. Two or three possibilities are still within the range of our capacity; beyond that, the waste of energy needed to make an assessment usually blocks the process completely. We prefer not to choose rather than to choose among innumerable possibilities. And that's not necessarily a bad thing. If we had to use our time to analyze the infinite choices that we are presented with all the time, our freedom of choice would not necessarily be increased as much as we might imagine.

Now consider the enormous number of living beings, nonhumans, with whom we share the planet. Plants alone account for 86.7 percent of life and fungi for 1.2 percent (that doesn't seem like much, but it is four times more than all the animals, which barely make up a miserable 0.3 percent); microorganisms make up the remainder.[2] The enormous number of other nonhuman living beings that share the planet with us is a factor capable of overloading our brain's capacity to process data, and then it becomes understandable why we *do not see* plants, fungi, or even animals, despite their similarity to us. If we do not see their organizational models, the ones that turn out to be winners from an evolutionary point of view, it is because our brain, thanks to its elementary and economical binary scheme, tends to simplify reality in order to bring it within the confines of its (low) capacity for calculation. We could never keep account of all these other forms of life and, indeed, we don't. We limit ourselves to excluding from the terms of any problem all of that which does not resemble ourselves. From blindness to blindness, we have thus eliminated so much intelligent life from our horizons that, in the end, we've found ourselves to be the only ones.

It's clear that such a distorted view of reality could not lead to anything good. Simplifying is always a good practice, but failing to consider the real terms of a problem is not. By removing nature from our gaze, we have begun to perceive ourselves as outside of or, worse, above it, well beyond the capacity of evolution to act on us. It is as though we thought we, rather than the vicissitudes of chance, could decide where and how our species is supposed to go. We have shared a certain stretch of the road with all the other species that populate this planet along with us, but unlike them, we have emancipated ourselves, maturing the firm conviction that the reins of our destiny are in our hands. Sure, every once in a while, some insignificant virus arrives to remind us that as long as we are born and (above all) die, we will always be part of nature. But despite these little mishaps, we remain convinced that we are the most evolved and complex being that ever walked the planet. That this is a mistaken idea, and that there is not any difference in the degree of evolution between us and all the other living beings on Earth, seems to us such a naïve idea that it isn't even worthy of rebuttal. So looking back on the exploits of humankind, great and small, often amounts, except for some minuscule but significant exceptions, to contemplating with devotion the only thing that we seem to be able to venerate: ourselves.

Therefore, at the top of the pyramid, the sole and exclusive uncontested lords of creation are humankind and, lower down, all the others in proportion to their greater or lesser vicinity to human perfection. Starting, obviously, with the primates (the name of the order, of which *Homo sapiens* is also a member, was coined by Linnaeus in 1758 and, not by chance, in Latin it means "the best") who are there, right next to us. They are not humans, certainly, but they share some characteristics that, not by chance, we believe to be fundamental in the description of our glory. From the 35 grams (1.2 ounces) of the mouse lemur of Madagascar to the 180 kilograms (400 pounds) of the gorilla, every primate is endowed with five fingers for each limb, with an opposable thumb and nails (not claws) so as to be able to solidly grasp branches and food; nonspecialized teeth typical of the omnivorous diet; binocular and color vision, with eyes pointing to the front so that the fields of vision overlap. But, above all, the main difference is that the weight of the primate brain, as a ratio of their body weight, is greater than that of the other terrestrial mammals.

In sum, even if primates are still not the light, they bear witness to it. Under the primates, in no particular order, we find all the other animals: First the mammals, then gradually the more distant birds, reptiles, amphibians, insects. Finally, at the base, confined in a faraway limbo that dissolves without pity into the inorganic world of minerals, with no brain or opposable thumbs, nor single or double organs, without even the capacity to move from place to place, there are the plants.

At the opposite end of the hierarchical scale that sees the light of humankind at its vertex lies the enormous mass of life, composed for the most part of defenseless plants, in contrast to the measureless power of our predatory capacity and without any value, except that we can recognize them as a resource for our survival. Their fixedness represents the very negation of the animal essence. Animal, in fact, means to be animated, to be able to move from place to place. Plants, with their rootedness, their inability to move from place to place, are as distant and different from animal life as one can imagine. It follows that, despite their constituting almost the totality of life on Earth, their being the very opposite of animal organization and functionality confines them to a place totally outside of the human horizon: invisible. We may think of plants as useful resources but certainly not as a life-form (even when they might be considered such) by which to be inspired for the design and construction of our magnificent works.

Every time I happen upon one of these scales of nature, designed in a way to demonstrate the absolute dominance of humankind over the life of a planet of which our species represents only a negligible portion, I can't help but associate this type of representation with those that illustrate the distribution of wealth among humans. You have certainly heard people talk about them: a minimal part of the human population possesses most of the wealth of the planet. This distribution is normally illustrated by a pyramid whose apex is represented by a minimal, if not laughable, percentage of the members of our species. There are various ways of analyzing this distribution of wealth. One of the most frequent comes to us from the work of Vilfredo Pareto, an Italian engineer and economist from the second half of the nineteenth century, who worked out a principle according to which, in a complex system, 20 percent of the causes provoke 80 percent of the effects. Applied to the economy, Pareto's principle illustrates, among other things, that 20 percent of the population possesses 80 percent of the wealth (and also that 0.8 percent possesses 51.2 percent). In 2023, a report by Oxfam revealed that the ten richest men on the planet possessed together more than the combined wealth of the

PEDIGREE OF MAN.

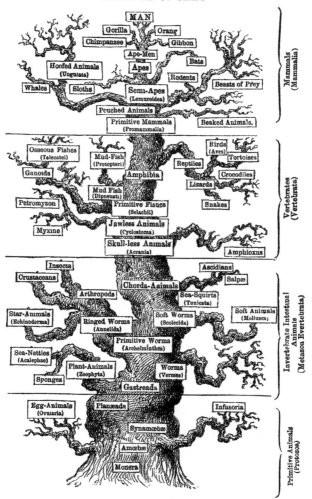

The *scala naturae* is a classic way of representing the order of the world, in which the internal hierarchy of nature starts from rocks, at the base, and goes all the way up to mankind, the apex of creation. The *scala naturae* is often portrayed as a ladder, sometimes, as in the case of this illustration taken from *The Evolution of Man* by Ernst Haekel, in the form of a genealogical tree at whose apex appears, as usual, man.

poorest 3.1 billion people.[3] In effect, ten people possessed the same wealth of almost half of the world's human population. It is such a strong and clear demonstration of the human drive to plunder well beyond any imaginable possible personal or group benefit that I don't believe it requires any further comment. We apply to other humans the same predatory norm that we apply to every other living being: No one is our peer and no one, beyond ourselves, is anything other than a resource to be possessed without any limit. A vision that we share with no other living species.

I once believed that plants and animals, by virtue of their total and irreconcilable opposition, were to be considered a bit like the yin and yang of life. I have been forced to change my view; for us, plants have never had any value at all. The human-animal-plant-mineral hierarchy, that rigid scale of nature, has always been adhered to.

I have recounted in greater detail on other occasions how the study of plants, despite its vast contributions to our knowledge about the functioning of life, hardly ever leads (the exceptions are truly exceptional) to any special recognition.[4] Cell theory, for example, which is fundamental to the field of biology, was born thanks to a discovery by Robert Hooke, who, by observing cork under a microscope, found that living organisms are composed of smaller units, cells, that are so named because of their similarity to the cells of monks. Another example is the heredity of characteristics, discovered by Gregor Mendel thanks to his legendary experiments on the crossbreeding of peas. In short, it is very difficult to overlook the importance of botany's discoveries for the progress of human knowledge, yet their importance is overlooked continuously.

Even Charles Darwin's theory of evolution is based for the most part on evidence coming from the vegetable kingdom. Darwin dedicated a large part of his life and works (some six volumes and seventy or so essays) to research on plants. Nonetheless, this enormous volume of work has always received much less attention than the rest of his research. As has been noted by Duane Isely, that Darwin wrote more about plants than he did about any other subject is certainly mentioned by scholars who have studied Darwin, "but it is casual," with a certain condescension, "something along the lines of 'Well, the great man needs to play now and then.'"[5]

That fundamental pillars of our understanding of life have been made possible by the studies done on plants doesn't seem to have any importance for the history of science. So it is that every discovery made in the vegetable kingdom continues to have only limited importance within the scientific community, until it is replicated and validated by a study on an animal species. Though it may be humble and distant from human experience, a nematode composed of 959 cells, the *Caenorhabditis elegans*, has been used in scientific experiments that have led to various Nobel Prizes. Its mere 302 neurons are enough to make it a reliable model. On the contrary, many fundamental biological discoveries made originally through the study of plants have had to be validated in this worm before they could be considered of universal value.

From science to philosophy, from economics to environmental protection, in every field of human activity, plants amount to nothing, a non-value. Let's take a very current theme like the defense of biodiversity. How many times have you heard about campaigns in favor of the rhinoceros, the koala, the panda, the monk seal, the Sardinian red deer, the giraffe, the blue whale, or the dolphin? There have been hundreds of them. To be sure, in perfect accordance with the scale of nature that we have been talking about, nearly all of these experiments involve mammals, along with a few birds and a very few amphibians (even though, practically speaking, they are extinct), reptiles, or fish. But what about plants? Have you ever heard about a campaign in favor of the Wollemi pine, the Paraná pine, Koyama's spruce, the American chestnut, the Sicilian zelkova, or the Sardinian columbine, all plants about to disappear forever? No. There doesn't exist even one, despite the enormous number of vegetable species on their way to extinction.

Now, I wouldn't want you to think that I have something against the Sardinian red deer or the monk seal. Helping them with consciousness-raising campaigns is important and just. But why concentrate all our (minuscule) ability to take care of living species on just animals? How is it that we are interested (only a little, let that be clear) in that miserable 0.3 percent of the biomass represented by animal life, while we do not believe to be of any interest the nearly 87 percent of life represented by plants? Yet, in purely self-interested terms, our life depends on plants, not on animals. We do not take care of them because they are there at the bottom, at the base of the pyramid, along with the great mass of life without a brain. So distant and incomprehensible as to be invisible. Simple resources, raw materials to be utilized, which have nothing to do with the complexity and superiority of animal life.

You're still not convinced? In 2022, I had a discussion with Giovanni Aloi—a professor at the School of the Art Institute of Chicago, who specializes in the representation of nature in modern and contemporary art—about the blindness toward plants in the artistic realm. Our discussion focused on the works of Lucian Freud, whom Aloi was studying on the occasion of the hundredth anniversary of his birth. Over the course of his career, Freud produced at least a hundred exquisite paintings that have plants as their subject. Yet, if it were not for the work of Aloi, which brought those paintings to the attention of critics and the general public on the occasion of his centenary, nobody would remember this, anything but marginal, part of Freud's production.[6]

Let's take as an example *Still Life with Aloe* (1949). Pictured on a white wood background are an aloe plant and a fish. The aloe, having just been uprooted, is painted with its roots bare, the hidden part of the plant immodestly exposed to our gaze. A plant out of the soil alongside a fish out of water; two living beings placed in a condition that makes their survival impossible. When I saw it for the first time, I thought about what might be an equivalent representation for a human—perhaps a body lying on the bottom of the sea. In any event, this splendid painting is only one of the hundred or so works in which Freud pictures plants. A magnificent and unknown pictorial corpus whose total lack of importance for the critics is shared by Freud's works and those of any other artist who has ever dreamed of entrusting to grasses, flowers, trees, and other vegetable subjects the manifestation of their art. This should come as no surprise; if Freud had limited himself to painting plants, no one would have celebrated his centennial. Indeed, the world of art continues to be subservient to the inviolable idea that there exists a hierarchy of nature in which humankind represents the apex of the pyramid and plants, along with stones and other inanimate objects, are the base.

Plants, landscapes, animals, single people, and, finally, groups of people, usually men or exalted men: this is the hierarchy of genres, as theorized in 1668 by André Félibien, the court historian to Louis XIV:

He who makes perfect landscapes is above another who only paints fruit, flowers, or seashells. He who paints living animals is worthier of estimation than those who paint only things that are dead and without movement. And as the figure of man is the most perfect work of God on Earth, it is also certain that he who becomes an imitator of God by painting human figures is much more excellent than all the others. However, even though it is no small thing to make the figure of a man appear as if alive, and to give the appearance of movement to that which has none, nevertheless a painter who only makes portraits...may not pretend to the honor accorded to the most learned. For that, it is necessary to progress from the single figure to the representation of several together, to depict history and myth...the virtue of great men and the most elevated mysteries.[7]

According to this theory of pictorial production, the still life—plants included, though they are totally alive—languishes at the bottom of this hierarchy, far below the highest art necessary for the reproduction of human portraits.

This history of Western civilization is marked by an obstinate indifference to the vast majority of living beings. Regardless of the passing of centuries, when it comes to studying plants, painting them, writing about them, or representing them, anyone involved is fated to irrelevance. And Freud would have suffered the same fate if his artistic production had been limited to the representation of plants. Bananas, thistles, tomatoes, sowbread, ferns, narcissus, lemons, yuccas, buttercups: Freud painted plants throughout his long career without any of his works of vegetable inspiration raising even minimal interest. Prior to Aloi's long-overdue contribution, the most the critics were able to express regarding the plants painted by Freud over the course of his career appears to have been this consideration of Lawrence Gowing regarding the yucca tree featured in *Interior at Paddington* (1951): "one of the most memorable potted plants in the history of modern art."[8] He doesn't explain why or add anything else; we must resign ourselves to this single observation. To my eyes, as I imagine to the eyes of anyone who has anything to do with plants, this amounts to an irreparable wrong.

To conclude, from Aristotle on, this ancient idea of the scale of the living has cheerfully passed through every epoch and affected every human activity, completely impermeable to the new revelations of science that have demonstrated, year after year, the marvelous capabilities, not only of plants but also of all of the other nonhuman beings that, along with us, populate our planet.

Two

THE BODY BECOMES ARCHITECTURE

Architecture has not avoided this anthropocentric fixation. It couldn't have. After all, it is one of the most human enterprises, which was created to satisfy some of the most basic biological needs of humankind, such as protection from atmospheric agents. By the sheer nature of things, architecture had to put humans at the center of all its activities. William Morris wrote: "My concept of architecture embraces the entire environment of human life; we cannot escape architecture as long as we are part of civilization, since it represents the set of modifications and alterations made on the earth's surface, in view of human needs, except for the pure desert."[1] It is not possible, therefore, to be inside civilization and escape from architecture, and with it from the human necessities that govern the design and functioning of our cities.

The *face* of the city to indicate its appearance, its *main artery*, green *lungs*, beating *heart*, the building *cells* that describe its different types of construction, and then its *nerve centers*, *structure*, *skin*: It is not difficult to see how these terms commonly used to describe cities underline the peculiar similarity and centrality that our body has in the design and organization used to shape urban centers. The entire history of architecture has been based on the dimensions and proportions of the human body. It is that body, in fact, which must find shelter in and move around inside buildings, and it is inevitable that it should be the measurements of that same body that regulate the dimensions, designs, and surfaces that are the stuff of architecture.

All you have to do is leaf through an architecture textbook or read the legal regulations that determine the dimensions of our homes to understand that it would not be possible to imagine a non-anthropocentric architecture. Taking into account human stature, a doorway is about 2.05 to 2.10 meters (6 feet, 6 inches to 7 feet) high. Since the width of human shoulders is about 0.55 meters (1 foot, 8 inches), a door must be at least 0.60 meters (2 feet) wide. Assuming that a man's outstretched arm is about 0.72 meters (2 feet, 4 inches) long, a man with an outstretched arm, including shoulders, occupies about 1.12 meters (3 feet, 8 inches), so a corridor that leaves some comfort is at least 1.20 meters (3 feet, 11 inches) wide. These are data that can be found everywhere and that demonstrate the obvious centrality of the human figure not only in architectural design but in the very way we perceive the city. It is a centrality that no one would ever dream of doubting and that in the Renaissance finds its maximum theoretical and artistic elaboration in Leonardo da Vinci's *Vitruvian Man*, so named in honor of the Roman architect Marcus Vitruvius on whose *De architectura* generations of architects were trained until the nineteenth century.

The Vitruvian man is in fact man as the measure of all things. Leonardo's drawing is a man of absolute proportions whose measurements are inscribed in the two perfect figures of the circle and the square. The circle is the symbol of Heaven while the square is the symbol of Earth. Man is represented as the symbol of the correspondence between the microcosm and the macrocosm.[2] On the drawing, Leonardo notes directly the relationship that exists between the proportions of his man and the harmonic proportions, for example, of the columns: "From the hairline to the bottom of the chin is one-tenth of the height of the man" in accordance with the passage from *De architectura* in which Vitruvius states that "posterity [established] that the height of the Doric columns was seven times their diameter."[3] In short, not only the measurements but also the proportions, the relations between the measurements, must be relative to man, the ultimate yardstick of everything.

Please don't get the idea that Vitruvius's notion of man as a unit of measurement is something that concerns a distant past. In 1950, in *Le modulor*,[4] the cover of which I found so beautiful as a boy that it made me fall in love with books as wonderful objects, Le Corbusier published a scale of proportions based on the measurements of man called, precisely, the Modulor. A fascinating story. First of all, the

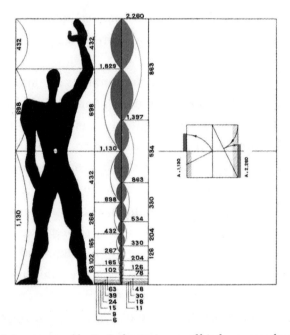

The Modulor, proposed by Le Corbusier in one of his famous works of 1950, is a scale of proportions based on the measurements of man. Its conception is part of a long tradition that, from Vitruvius onward, sees the use of the relationships of the human body as one of the surest ways to improve the beauty and functionality of architectural projects.

name itself reveals Le Corbusier's architectural conception: The word "Modulor" comes from the union of the French words *module* and *or* ("golden" as in *section d'or*, that is, the golden ratio), and recalls the desire to create an instrument capable of bringing the measurements of the human body back to the proportions of the golden ratio, a very recurrent proportion in nature that, as such, humans perceive as pleasurable.

Le Corbusier, like every architect since time immemorial, knew that defining architectural measurements on the dimensions of the golden ratio produced aesthetically pleasing solutions. He thus divides the human body into three intervals—from the foot to the solar plexus, from the solar plexus to the top of the head, from the head to the fingertips of a hand raised above the head—whose ratios are equal to the golden ratio (whose value is equal to 1.62) and creates two series. The red series is based on the average height of the European man, which Le Corbusier sets at 1.75 meters (5 feet, 9 inches), from which derives a height of the solar plexus of 1.08 meters (3 feet, 6 inches), completely in line with what is predicted by the golden ratio (if we divide 1.75 by 1.08, we get the fateful 1.62 of the golden ratio). Subsequently, the average height was reset to 1.83 meters (6 feet) with a consequent increase in the height of the solar plexus to 1.13 meters (3 feet, 8 inches)—still the golden ratio.

The second series, called the blue series, was later based by Le Corbusier on the height of a man with his arm raised, whose measurement from the tips of his fingers stretched above his head to the ground was fixed at 2.26 meters (7 feet, 5 inches) and from which, using the golden ratio, it was possible to derive every other dimension of the human body.

With the Modulor, Le Corbusier thus created an instrument that could easily provide "a range of harmonious measures to satisfy the human dimension, universally

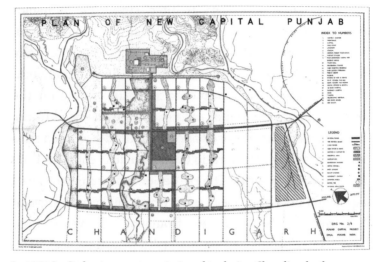

In 1951 Le Corbusier was commissioned to design Chandigarh, the new capital of Punjab. At first glance, the layout of the city imagined by Le Corbusier appears to be quite different from the organization of a human body. However, if you look carefully, you will notice numerous similarities. All the functions of government and administration are concentrated in the rectangular area represented in gray at the top (the head); the main roads are described as arteries; the business district is in the heart of the city.

applicable to architecture and mechanical things"[5] and which he would use often in the design of all his works. Among these, the most important is undoubtedly the city of Chandigarh in India, the formidable project of the new capital of Punjab that Prime Minister Nehru entrusted to Le Corbusier in the early 1950s. With the Modulor at his disposal, and with the very solid idea he shared with Vitruvius, Leonardo, and Alberti that man is the perfect form and organization to be inspired in design, Le Corbusier designed a city of wide boulevards arranged in a grid to connect the fifty-six sectors into which the city is divided.

At first glance, the urban plan of Chandigarh would seem to be inspired only by criteria of practicality and not at all by the organization of the human body. But if we study the plan of this city in detail, we find that it is drawn exactly like a human body (or animal if you prefer). As Kapil Setia, Chandigarh's chief architect of urban planning, eloquently recounted, Le Corbusier's project is entirely comparable to a human body, "with the most important buildings, those of the capital, at the head, the central business district as the heart, the industrial areas on the eastern flank and those of education on the opposite side, as if they were the two arms of the city."[6] The three grandiose buildings that Le Corbusier designed to house the governing bodies—the Palace of Justice, the Palace of Assembly, the Secretariat—are thus all located in the head area, to control the body of the city that he imagines in accordance with the same organization as a human body. And this is what we read in the report of a meeting of the Chandigarh design team, reported by Peter Hall in *Cities of Tomorrow*: "Corbusier held a crayon in his hand and he was in his element. '*Voilà la gare*,' he said, '*et voici la rue commercial*,' and drew the first street on the new plain of Chandigarh. '*Voici la tête*,' he continued, pointing with a slap to an area higher [...] '*Et voilà l'estomac, le cité-centre*.'"[7]

Before Chandigarh, in 1930, Le Corbusier had worked on the design of another ideal city: the Ville Radieuse. Although never realized, it too was organized hierarchically around the idea of the human body. The Ville Radieuse project combines the idea of a linear city with the abstract image of a man: head, spine, arms, and body. The skyscrapers are arranged in the head and the body is made up of acres of residential strips. What is striking is that Le Corbusier adopts this anthropomorphic design strategy precisely to escape from a purely geometric design. The geometrical order of the grid is contrasted with the natural order expressed by the biological analogy: The nerve center of business is the head, the residential areas are the lungs, the cultural center is the heart, and, finally, the feet represent heavy industry.

According to Le Corbusier, it is biology that pushes toward the separation of organs and functions, both in the body and in the city. This makes it an inescapable principle. In the 1960s he wrote: "A design arranges the organs in order, thus creating one or more organisms. BIOLOGY! The great new word of architecture and urban planning."[8]

He was right, biology is really the new word of urban planning. What was wrong was to limit biology to the animal form alone. On the other hand, Le Corbusier was not the first, nor would he be the last, to be inspired by what we human beings perceive as the sum of perfection, not only aesthetic but also functional: our body. Its centralized organization, with a head that governs single or double specialized organs, we find practically in the design of every city on the planet. From the oldest to the most recent—whether it is the city of Ur, Athens, or Rome, whose current maps record the passing of millennia, or any of the many new cities designed from scratch, starting from a blank sheet of paper and a colored pencil, as in the case of Le Corbusier's Chandigarh—in each of them we will find the more or less clear idea of a city designed to work as a human body works. In some cases, the inspiration is declared and explicit, even more so than in the case of Chandigarh; other times it is the inevitable consequence of the stratification of thousands of years of human history and adherence to the only model of organization that we know.

Take, for example, one of the most compelling known representations of the anthropomorphic city. We owe it to Francesco di Giorgio Martini, a Sienese architect and theorist, whose notes of merit include his having introduced Leonardo to the work of Vitruvius. In the second half of the fifteenth century, Francesco wrote *A Treatise on Civil and Military Architecture*, which depicts a magnificent example of a city built on the design of the human body. In the explanations accompanying the drawing, Francesco explains:

> The city, the fortress and the castle should be modeled on the form of a human body, the head with its attached members should have a proportionate correspondence, and the head should be the fortress, the arms its recessed walls which, turning around it, connect it to the rest of the whole body...And therefore, it should be considered that just as the body has all its members and parts in perfect measurements and proportions,

in the composition of temples, cities, fortresses, and
castles the same principles should be observed.

This is the first theoretical elaboration on the need to design cities in accordance with human organization. The representation is impressive in its clarity: The head is the seat
of power (the fortress), the temple is the heart, the square is
the stomach, the arms and legs its defensive towers. Francesco's vision of the city is organized on the perfection of
the human body, which, more or less consciously, would
forever accompany every urban planner who would ever be
asked to imagine and plan a new city.

Let's also consider the myriad of ideal cities designed
from the Renaissance onward. From Pienza to Urbino, from
Sabbioneta in Lombardy to Acaya in Puglia, there have been
countless attempts to create a city whose geometry reflects
in its forms, in the hierarchy of the layout of its streets
and squares, that celestial harmony that Leonardo drew in
the form of his *Vitruvian Man*. The tradition of ideal cities, inaugurated by Thomas More with his *Utopia*, has never
ceased to exert its fascination: chessboard or star layouts,
wide streets, buildings homogeneous in size and style. City
design has thus become a real genre, and from the Renaissance to the present day every architect with a high opinion
of his ideas has felt compelled to design their ideal city. The
fact that they all tend to resemble each other, as real cities
do, doesn't seem to bother anyone. Try taking a look at their
plans. What changes is the shape, which can be a square,

a star with or without spikes, a polyhedron, or any other regular and symmetrical geometric figure. Otherwise, symmetrical streets branching off from a center, where the government building, the church, the barracks, and possibly services are located. That's it. In the most refined of these representations, the areas of the city are specialized in particular functions: cultural, industrial, health care, etc. In short, the good old organization of our animal body, re-proposed in different sauces but without any significant variation: always a center/head, around which revolve specialized areas/organs on which the survival of the city depends. The fact that they are theoretical creations produced from the only model of organization with which we are familiar makes them all merely minimal variations on the theme of the animal body. Moreover, if we really are on the lookout for innovations, we're much more likely to find them in real, rather than ideal, cities.

The reason is simple: In living cities, over the course of their history, dimensional growth and urban development are the fruit of choices made by successive generations, who soon learn to be flexible enough to escape rigid urban planning constraints, reacquiring that disorder typical of natural growth, in which it is evolution that decides, from among the thousands of possible solutions, the one that is most suitable.

Suitable: This is the adjective around which everything revolves. Evolution always rewards the *most suitable* solution, not the best, which, on the contrary, is a purely human

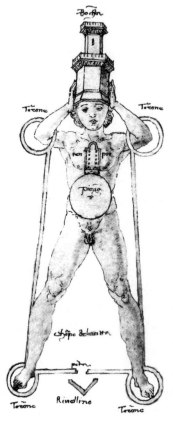

In the second half of the fifteenth century, Francesco di Giorgio Martini wrote *A Treatise on Civil and Military Architecture*, in which appears this magnificent image of a fortified citadel drawn on the form of a human figure. In Francesco's design, the inspiration from the human body, the perfect organization on which to design each of our creations, manifests itself in all its power.

obsession. Every planned city is, of course, the best according to the intentions of its designer, but designing an entire city in every detail is as difficult a matter as designing an entire living being. There are so many factors that coexist and that vary in unpredictable ways. To design a living city from scratch, one would have to believe that one is similar to God. Thus, every time an architect, devoid of shame or

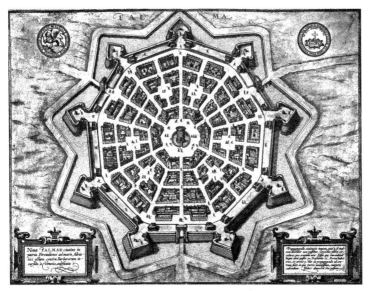

The fortress city of Palmanova was founded at the end of the sixteenth century by the Republic of Venice to defend its eastern borders, in order to counter the Turkish threat and the territorial expansion of the Habsburgs across the low Friulian plain. With its nine-point star shape, its eighteen sides with protruding and recessed corners, each corresponding to a bulwark, Palmanova is one of the most extraordinary achievements of an ideal city.

doubts, plays the role of Architect, the results are always terrible. Planned cities are inert urban elaborations. The theoretical nature of reflection makes them cold, inhospitable, unsuitable for organic life. Some of these monsters have been made and inhabited, and they have their admirers. To me, every time I have visited one of them, they give me the impression of a mausoleum, of a grandiose and monumental tomb. Rational, but lifeless. It is the life of the city that makes it beautiful, through the continual choice of the most suitable solutions dictated by the laws of evolution.

It is no coincidence that many of the ideal cities that have had the opportunity to move from paper to reality have been able to do so for reasons that are anything but ideal, but rather very practical. The uniformity of the spaces, the hierarchical layout of the plan, the roles assigned to the different urban areas, the rationality of the streets are all concepts that are highly appreciated in some specific environments—for example, military life. Thus, cities such as Palmanova or Sforzinda are cities that have nothing of the ideal at all, except for the military that created real strongholds there, so much so that the starry shape became a model for the fortresses of half of Europe. Another, Terra del Sole, commissioned by Cosimo I de' Medici in Romagna, on the border of his duchy, despite its name and the pleasantness of its design, has nothing ideal about it. It was mostly used as a prison, whose remains include the ghastly graffiti of its inmates.

I don't think it's a coincidence that the panopticon, the prison designed at the end of the eighteenth century by Jeremy Bentham, in its own way also a small ideal city, is one of the most successful designs. The concept behind the panopticon, a circular building built around a central tower, was to allow a single guard, thanks to the building's radiocentric shape, to be able to observe (*optikon*) all (*pan*) the prisoners at all times. According to the designer, the fact that they were always under control would induce in the

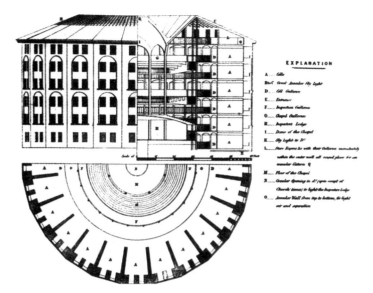

The design of the panopticon is by Jeremy Bentham, an English philosopher from the late eighteenth and early nineteenth centuries. Known as one of the first exponents of utilitarianism, Bentham envisaged a model prison built on a circular plan so that each of the cells in the entire prison could be visible—or considered as such by prisoners—to a single person posted inside a central observation structure.

prisoners the perception of a sort of omniscience on the part of the warden, leading them to obey.

Throughout history, much of this drive for idealism in urban design has often been reduced to little more than an efficient organization of cities that facilitates their control.

Three

THE EVOLVING CITY

That the city can be studied as a living organism subject to the rules of life and evolution is an old story dating back to at least the second half of the nineteenth century. That is when Patrick Geddes, a Scottish botanist born in 1854 and one of the founding fathers of urbanism, began to theorize that cities and their planning should be treated in evolutionary terms. It was inevitable that this would happen. There was no way Geddes could remain immune to the revolutionary fascination of the theory of evolution. The years of his youth were the years in which Darwin's theory of evolution (*On the Origin of Species* was published for the first time on November 24, 1859) literally changed the world, explaining much more than the way in which species originated and evolved, and providing a new key to understanding the whole of reality. In addition, from 1874 to 1879 Geddes studied in London with the influential philosopher and biologist Thomas Huxley, one of the most fervent supporters of evolutionism, so much so that he earned the nickname "Darwin's Bulldog." In his autobiography, Darwin wrote enthusiastically of Huxley:

His mind is as quick as a flash of lightning and as sharp
as a razor. He is the best talker whom I have known.
He never writes and never says anything flat. From his
conversation no one would suppose that he could cut
up his opponents in so trenchant a manner as he can
do and does do. He has been a most kind friend to me
and would always take any trouble for me. [...] He is
a splendid man and has worked well for the good of
mankind.[1]

It was impossible not to come out of Huxley's school with a
strong evolutionary education.

Geddes participated in the Darwinian revolution and
fully shared its conclusions, including the new light it threw
on any field of human knowledge. It seemed perfectly designed to describe even something as old as a city in a new
way. All that was needed was someone to translate Darwin's discoveries into urban planning. This someone was
Geddes, whose book *Cities in Evolution* (1915) expounds the
idea that the city should be conceived not as a set of inorganic structures assembled by man but as an organism
whose development is determined by the environment in
which it lives and which has, in turn, a direct influence on
the environment that surrounds it. A city that is like "the
spreadings of a great coral reef. Like this, it has a stony skel-
eton, and living polypes—call it, then, a 'man-reef' if you
will."[2] Today, the analogy between cities and living beings
may be quite familiar, but at the time it was a real revolution. Geddes, with his evolutionary approach, became the

interpreter of a new way of conceiving urban planning—an integrated activity capable of understanding the needs of a living city. "Cities [are] living organisms; [they] are born and...develop, disintegrate and die. [...] In its academic and traditional sense, city planning has become obsolete. In its place must be substituted urban biology," the architect and urban planner José Luís Sert would declare in 1942 during the Congrès Internationaux d'Architecture Moderne.[3] But although we know that studying and understanding the metabolism and catabolism of cities would have fundamental consequences for the environment and lead to huge improvements in their efficiency, Geddes's vision, which would have all the characteristics to change modern urban planning, has not made inroads.

A share of the responsibility for this failed revolution lies with Geddes himself, who had his own original interpretation of evolution which, at the time he wrote, could have been considered not to be in perfect conformity with Darwinian orthodoxy. But the differences were mere details, and most of his beliefs about evolution, which he suggested should be applied to urban planning theory, are perfectly in keeping with Darwinian theory. He embraced the idea that humans are part of evolution and that their evolutionary history has shaped every single one of their behaviors; that cities are equivalent to complex organisms whose adaptive behaviors evolve and adapt to the environment in a de facto autonomous way, largely beyond the control of their planners; that the environment of the city itself influences and can act on the social and cultural evolution of its inhabitants. Nevertheless, what went against social Darwinist orthodoxy was Geddes's emphasis on theorizing the importance of cooperation in the development of cities, as opposed to the struggle for existence that was held to be one of the fundamental thrusts of evolution, the only one Darwinianly acceptable. The fact that a pupil of Huxley, the main popularizer of the idea that life is nothing but a continuous struggle in which only a few survive, allowed himself to have such a heterodox conception of evolution was never forgiven.

It must be borne in mind that for Huxley, the concept of the struggle for existence, which Darwin uses in a predominantly metaphorical way, represents the true and tangible natural counterpart of the "situation of continuous struggle," described by Thomas Hobbes in *Leviathan*, which induces men to place themselves "in the state and posture of *gladiators* having their *weapons pointing*, and their *eyes fixed on one another*."[4] We owe to Huxley the widespread use of the image of the gladiator as the one that most closely adheres to an idea of evolution in which, outside of "limited and temporary family relations, the Hobbesian war of all against all" constitutes "the normal model of existence."[5] A position that was very popular and was promptly adopted and spread by the social Darwinists. In a brief time, the image of life as an arena of gladiators engaged in slaughtering each other would become the banal and erroneous representation by which the theory of evolution would be known to most people. A vision that would produce, and unfortunately continues to produce, enormous harm and that would see, in Geddes's time, only very few intellectuals publicly challenge it.

One of these characters, relevant to our history because he was linked to Geddes by feelings of mutual esteem and friendship,[6] is Élisée Reclus, a well-known French geographer and the author, between 1876 and 1894, of the monumental *Nouvelle géographie universelle*. A fierce critic of the social Darwinists and their gladiatorial vision of life, he wrote of them: "They say this with a kind of rage, as if the sight of blood excited them to murder."[7] Indeed, his idea of evolution, which he fully shares with Geddes, is very different. Reclus does not emphasize the evolution of the fittest through the individual tooth-and-nail struggle but through the value of solidarity, thanks to which we witness the association of spontaneous and coordinated forces that lead to progress. He writes that

the law of the blind and brutal struggle for existence, so exalted by the worshippers of success, is subordinated to a second law, that of the grouping of weak individuals into ever more developed organisms, which learn to defend themselves against enemy forces, to recognize the resources of their environment, even to create new ones. We know that if our descendants attain their high destiny of science and freedom, they will owe it to their ever more intimate coming together, to their unceasing collaboration, to this mutual aid from which brotherhood gradually grows.[8]

It is to this type of evolution that Geddes refers with his evolutionary conception of the city, an evolution that does not act through the relentless struggle of all against all but instead draws its fundamental strength from the cooperation between its inhabitants. From the important research of the biologist Lynn Margulis onward, we know that this vision is supported by solid scientific evidence.[9] In fact, cooperation, mutual support, or, as we say today, symbiosis is truly one of the fundamental engines of evolution, whose power acts without distinction on individuals and communities, all the way up to the development of cities.

In addition to the friendship with Reclus, an important contribution to Geddes's elaboration of his intuition about the importance of cooperation as a factor in evolution also came from Pyotr Alekseyevich Kropotkin, whom Geddes knew personally and respected. In 1902, the Russian prince Kropotkin—a philosopher, scientist, one of the fathers of anarchist thought, and, above all, a great evolutionary biologist and opponent of Huxley's simplistic theses—published a fundamental book entitled *Mutual Aid: A Factor of Evolution*, whose first paragraph reads:

Two aspects of animal life impressed me most during the journeys which I made in my youth in Eastern Siberia and Northern Manchuria. One of them was the extreme severity of the struggle for existence which most species of animals have to carry on against an inclement Nature; the enormous destruction of life which periodically results from natural agencies; and the consequent paucity of life over the vast territory which fell under my observation. And the other was, that even in those few spots where animal life teemed in abundance, I failed to find—although I was eagerly looking for it—that bitter struggle for the means of existence, *among animals belonging to the same species*, which was considered by most Darwinists (though not always by Darwin himself) as the dominant characteristic of struggle for life, and the main factor of evolution.[10]

In his book, Kropotkin argues for a suggestive thesis that has fundamental relevance to urban theory. In fact, he writes that in his numerous travels to some of the most inhospitable areas of the planet he has almost never found among the vegetable, animal, and human populations of those areas behaviors that could be described as competitive or, in general, in conformity with that idea of the arena in which the most fearsome survives. On the contrary, what seemed evident to him was that there was a widespread and conscious predisposition toward mutual support and that in extreme environments, as in the case of Siberia, the only chances of survival for any living organism lay in full and unconditional collaboration with all the other individuals of its own species and, often, with those of other species.

Certainly not in competition. Kropotkin also writes that, as far as he has seen in his travels, competition between individuals has a chance to exist only when there is a concomitance of two very important factors: a favorable and stable environment combined with a wealth of resources. When one of these requirements is not met, cooperation, or rather mutual aid, is by far the most efficient and, therefore, evolution-driven system for ensuring survival.

This is an extraordinary insight that seems to go against common sense. It is precisely in scarcity of resources that we would imagine the greatest competition, not in conditions of abundance. How many times have we thought that men or animals who fight fiercely to secure the few resources available are the blatant representation of the need to compete to survive? The ethic of the gladiator, in which only one remains alive: the strongest. Kropotkin, thanks to his punctual observations and his treatise's myriad of well-documented examples, provides for the first time the scientific evidence to support the idea that cooperation is a fundamental driver of evolution. His is an intuition that we not only know to be true but that in an era like ours, characterized by an unstable environment (such as that typically induced by global warming) and declining resources, takes on an even more exceptional relevance for the way we imagine and build our cities.

We can say with certainty that the emphasis on synergy and cooperation that distinguishes Geddes's writings on the city is fully supported by current scientific knowledge.

From this point of view, his observance of the precepts of evolution is sound. Where, on the other hand, his orthodoxy is somewhat shaky, so much so that it is incompatible with Darwinian teaching, is when Geddes suggests that urban evolution should be imagined as a gradual unfolding of a sort of development program inherent in the city itself. In fact, Darwinian evolution denies this very idea: There is no purpose to evolution, nor a model to be attained; not even an increase in complexity, as we sometimes hear. There is no such thing: Evolution cannot be predicted because change can move in any direction. All we can be sure of is that evolution will continue to work unabated, adapting species, as well as cities, to the conditions of a changing environment.

One of the fundamental ideas of evolutionary theory that Geddes does not understand, or perhaps does not accept, is that a combination of tiny changes, often completely disconnected from one another, can lead to a great change. This is one of Darwin's most powerful insights: Small, random changes can lead to the emergence of a new order. Evolution does not operate through upheavals but through small, gradual changes.

This is one of the most valuable lessons for urban planners: The destiny of a city is not in the exclusive hands of any architectural firm or administrative office but in the activities of its citizens, who, with each of their daily actions and choices over the middle and long term, imperceptibly modify its structure. From this point of view, the

In January 1868 Charles Darwin published *The Variation of Animals and Plants Under Domestication*. The pigeons shown here represent only some of the many variations that can be observed among the numerous breeds selected by humans. Like pigeons, cities vary greatly from one another while maintaining a perfectly recognizable structure.

work of those who are called upon to imagine the future of our cities must consider the inescapable force of evolution. An architect could learn so much from reading Darwin's *The Variation of Animals and Plants Under Domestication*! And yet, it almost seems that many urban planners are among the last creationists in circulation, the last still convinced of the creative power of *design*.

Every ideal city or building, finally, seems to be only an exercise of power: a perfect city but contrary to nature, an expression of the will to dominate. It is precisely for this reason that animal organization—centralized, hierarchical, delimited—finds in these ideal cities the apex of its use. A city in which the governing bodies are grouped at its center and specialized is very easy to control; having control over the few organs of power and decision-making is enough to govern the entire city. That removing or eliminating those same few organs of power is enough to destroy the entire government of the city is a reminder of the inherent weakness of any organization centralized in the way of animal organization. And it is precisely the question of the extreme fragility of our cities that is of the greatest importance for all of us today.

Four

THE SURVIVAL OF THE FITTEST

ANIMALS

So much are cities subject to evolution that they can really be compared to living beings. Even more than that, they are themselves a strong impetus for the evolution of the species that populate them. The environment of the city is so peculiar and, in many ways, extreme, that the selective pressure it exerts on living beings can produce significant changes in the structure and behavior of plants, animals, and microorganisms at a speed that was previously not thought possible. The study of this phenomenon is one of the most interesting and fascinating fields of research for understanding how evolution works.

To better understand what we are talking about, it is worth pausing for a moment on the meaning of a word that we will often find cited in the following pages and of which it is necessary to have as precise an idea as possible. The term *ecosystem* was first used in 1935 in a well-known essay by the British botanist Arthur Tansley,[1] although it was coined, at his request, by another botanist, Arthur

Roy Clapham. Tansley believed that organisms cannot be separated from the environment in which they live, "with which they form a single physical system." Ecosystems, therefore, are considered the "basic units of nature" and are of the "most varied types and sizes." Moreover, Tansley notes that, although organisms are considered the most important parts of these systems, inorganic factors are also fundamental because "there is constant interchange of the most various kinds within each system, not only between the organisms, but also between the organic and the inorganic."[2] The meaning of *ecosystem*, although it has undergone slight variations over time, is that of an ecological system (short form: "ecosystem"), consisting of all the organisms that populate it and the physical environment with which they interact. Organisms and the physical environment are inextricably linked through nutrient cycles and energy flows.

Now that we have a clear idea of what an ecosystem is, we can say that the city, which we have so far compared to a living being, is actually an ecosystem made up of all the organisms that live there (including humans) and the physical environment of streets, buildings, uncultivated land, water, etc. Its characteristics, regardless of where it is geographically located or how it is built or how ancient it is, are always rather constant.

The urban ecosystem has a whole series of characteristics that make it unique. In fact, not only is it home to more than half of the human population but it is also arguably the fastest-growing ecosystem on the planet. The rapid expansion of such a particular ecosystem, characterized by homogeneous environmental factors such as high temperatures, scarce vegetation, pollution, more impermeable surfaces, fragmented habitats divided by roads and buildings, replicated so many times in every region of the planet, at completely different climates and latitudes, represents a perfect laboratory in which to analyze how evolution works. It should not be surprising that the study of what happens to the species that share the urban environment with us, which until a few decades ago was of interest only to a very small group of researchers, has in recent years become an inescapable field of study in every serious biology laboratory on the planet. The results have not been long in coming; from rats to sparrows, from *Taraxacum officinale* (dandelions or blowballs, as you prefer) to clover, from mosquitoes to water fleas, there doesn't seem to be a species that has not been directly or indirectly involved in this enormous evolutionary experiment that is life in the city.

The forerunner of all research on the evolution of living species as a result of the evolutionary pressure generated by humans, and also one of the most famous and cited studies to explain how evolution works, concerns the change of color of a particular English butterfly, the birch moth, *Biston betularia*, in response to coal pollution. In a famous paper published in 1955, the British geneticist Bernard Kettlewell studied the two forms of this moth present in Great Britain, a white form called *typica* and a black one

The *Biston betularia* is a moth that exists in a light form called *typica* and a dark form called *carbonaria*. Its name derives from its habit of perching on the trunks of birch trees (*Betula*). The moth is known to be a clear proof of the theory of evolution: The population, composed almost exclusively of light individuals, became composed almost exclusively of dark individuals starting in the nineteenth century due to pollution that changed its habitat by blackening the trees on which they rested.

called *carbonaria*, wondering why in some areas of Britain one type was more widespread, while in others the opposite was true.[3] Precisely, in the natural areas less affected by coal-dust pollution, the white form (*typica*), which camouflaged itself perfectly with the light trunk of the birch and with the white lichens that were found on its trunk, was prevalent. In this natural situation, the few dark butterflies (*carbonaria*) present, standing out on the white trunk of the trees, became easy prey for birds, which thus limited their propagation. The opposite was true in urban areas or, in any case, in very polluted areas, close to cities. Here the coal dust covered every surface, including the trunks of the

trees, highlighting the white form, and perfectly camou-
flaging the black one. In these areas it was, of course, the
white form that was preyed upon by birds, leaving the black
form free to multiply. In the years following Kettlewell's
study, very stringent regulations on carbon particle emissions came into force in Britain. As a result of these laws,
which significantly decreased the incidence of soot pollution, the trees returned to their original brightness and,
shortly thereafter, the moth populations also adapted to
the restoration of the original situation, through an increase in the population of white moths. In short, thanks to
the birch moth, we have not only a clear example of how a
change in the environment induced by the work of humans
in urban contexts can directly affect the evolution of other
species that share the same environment with us but also
a magnificent example of how the survival of the fittest is
not predictable a priori, because it depends on changes in
the environment.

Whether they are animals or plants, most city-dwelling
species are quickly adapting their bodies and habits to the
new urban environment. The number of modifications that
can be useful in the city is enormous, from the smaller
teeth in New York rats to the mosquitoes that have adapted
to living inside the London Underground, from clover that
reduces its defenses against predators to the thousands of
adaptations of city birds. These are changes that strike our
imagination because of the familiarity we have with these
species and for the plasticity they demonstrate in adapting

to the urban ecosystem. However, most of the changes that urban species face are more hidden, less compelling, and have to do with their ability to withstand, as far as possible, human-made disasters.

A very common fish in aquariums around the world is the killifish. These are little fish, whose strange name is thought to derive from the Dutch word *kil*, "stream." Stream fish, and indeed most of the many species that are generally known as killifish, live in fresh or brackish waters. The interest in these fish, or rather in a particular killifish, the *Fundulus heteroclitus* that lives along the Atlantic coast of the United States, was sparked in the 1980s by the observations of researchers working for the Environmental Protection Agency in some of the most polluted sites in North America. Many of these sites contained perfectly healthy killifish that were able to swim in some of the most hydrocarbon-polluted waters ever seen. This was inexplicable, as killifish were considered a species very sensitive to hydrocarbon pollution.

If there was one thing the researchers were sure of, it was that they wouldn't find killifish in certain places. Specifically, those sites polluted by high concentrations of polycyclic aromatic hydrocarbons, polychlorinated biphenyls—that is, large classes of chemicals extremely common in oil spills or industrial pollution, to which very few living beings were able to develop a resistance. These are all common pollutants in urban environments. Well, what was most striking in the studies published following

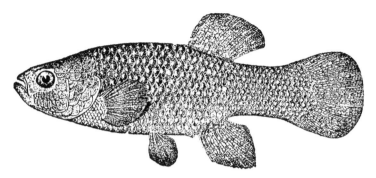

Fundulus heteroclitus is a small fish that inhabits the brackish coastal waters of the United States and Canada. It is a species known for its hardiness because it is able to tolerate variable salinity, temperatures in the range of 6° to 35°C (43° to 97°F), and very low oxygen levels. Recently, studies have shown that this species is able to survive in areas heavily polluted by compounds such as dioxins or hydrocarbons, codifying more than 20 percent of its genes.

those observations was the incredible increase in the resistance of killifish to these substances. Within a few decades, populations of killifish had formed that could easily withstand concentrations of these pollutants six thousand times higher than levels they survived in the past.[4]

At first glance it would seem to be a magnificent result, capable of giving us hope in the ability of species to adapt even to the most disastrous changes in the environment, such as those that we humans can make. But what happened to the killifish is something that can hardly be repeated. One of the reasons why these fish have been able to develop resistance to these pollutants is that they come from populations of enormous size and with a genetic

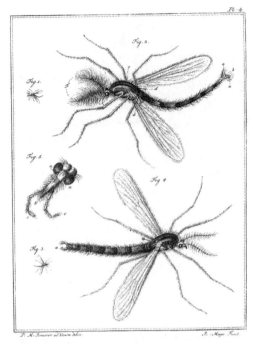

Culex pipiens mosquitoes are distributed in every corner of the planet. The males of the genus *Culex* are harmless and feed on nectar, while females suck the blood of vertebrates, especially mammals and birds, to develop their eggs. A subspecies of *Culex pipiens* has developed in the London Underground. It is perfectly adapted to this new environment and feeds only on human blood.

diversity that cannot be compared with that of any other vertebrate. In many urban estuaries, killifish are the most common vertebrate species, with many millions of individuals per estuary. Such huge populations of animals are carriers of enormous genetic diversity, which also includes the solution capable of making them resistant to many pollutants. When these populations came into contact with the polluted sites, all the nonresistant individuals died and only a very few lucky carriers of particularly favorable mutations survived. In a way, the killifish managed to survive because it already held the solution in its deck of cards, but many other species with smaller populations—with a smaller deck of cards—would never be able to do likewise. For all these other species, the levels of pollution that killifish can resist today means extinction.

Another example of fascinating urban evolution, for the place where it occurred and the species it involved, is the case of the London Underground mosquitoes. *Culex molestus* is a peculiar mosquito, a relative of the common mosquito from which it would seem (there is no conclusive evidence) to have deviated genetically since it found itself isolated in the tunnels of the London Underground. It adapted so well that, during the air raids on London during the Second World War, its ravenous bites were among the discomforts most cited by people seeking shelter from the bombings inside the Central Line and Piccadilly Circus stations. In the 1990s, the University of London geneticist Katharine Byrne, by joining the underground maintenance teams, managed to collect mosquito samples from the tunnels of three different tube lines—Central, Bakerloo, and Victoria—and found that these populations were not only different from each other but also distinguished from mosquitoes of the same species that lived on the surface.[5] Their habits, Menno Schilthuizen tells us in his fine volume on the evolution of species in the urban environment, were quite different.[6] Surface mosquitoes have a diet that includes the blood of birds as well as human blood, and before laying eggs they follow a characteristic procedure: Females must eat a blood-based meal, gather in large swarms to mate, and then hibernate. What happens with their underground peers is completely different. In the subway, mosquitoes suck only people's blood, lay eggs before eating, mate in small dark spaces, do not form any breeding swarms, and are active year-round. Seeing the speed with which living organisms change their behavior to adapt to man-made environments should once again make us understand that our actions, for example the proliferation of urban environments, have an irreversible effect on life, a responsibility that at the moment does not seem, in any way, to interest us.

One of the key challenges in the study of these adaptations is the question of whether these are simple adaptations or true evolution. The issue is by no means simple. In the case of the London Underground mosquitoes, for example, the discussion is open, and it has yet to be decided whether they are new species or simply different populations of the same species. It might seem like a classic controversy for experts in the field, with little interest for laymen. But it's not so much a question of whether the subway mosquito should be given a different name from the others but of knowing something that we have yet to find out, that is, the speed at which evolution might work. Is it really a phenomenon that proceeds by tiny random mutations and therefore requires countless generations before a new species can be formed? Or, on the contrary, are there aspects that still elude us and that could make the phenomenon occur much faster? To answer such a fundamental question, the commitment of generations of scientists will be necessary, but a significant contribution could come from studies on urban ecosystems. This is why it is essential to distinguish between the two responses that living organisms can put in place to respond to altered environments: evolution, that is, the genetic alterations that appear over generations, or simple phenotypic plasticity, which, despite the uncongenial name, is simply the ability to alter physical characteristics or behaviors in the course of a lifetime. In other words, are subway mosquitoes genetically different from surface mosquitoes, or have they just gotten used to living underground? These are the questions where our understanding of how evolution works is at stake.

An organism about which there seems to be no doubt, and which is believed to have effectively mutated to adapt to an urban environment, is the water flea, *Daphnia magna*. A tiny freshwater crustacean a few millimeters long, the water flea demonstrates an astonishing ability to evolve in cities in response to heat, pollution, and even local predators. To be honest, the water flea is the perfect example of the coexistence of adaptive changes by way of phenotypic plasticity and evolution proper: If you breed water fleas at higher temperatures—such as those found in urban bodies of water, compared to rural areas—you will notice that the crustaceans tend to be smaller and that they mature and reproduce more quickly; a classic example of phenotypic plasticity.[7] However, over time, water fleas that live stably, generation after generation, in warmer urban ponds have varied their genetic makeup, and this is evolution.[8]

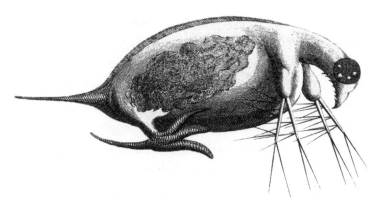

Water fleas, such as the one pictured here, are tiny crustaceans belonging to the genus *Daphnia*, ranging from less than one to five millimeters long. These little animals live in pools, ponds, and rivers and are considered indicators of the health of waterways. Water fleas that grow in an urban environment have adapted to the new conditions, and in cities they exhibit rapid maturation, early release of progeny, and dimensions smaller than their rural counterparts.

When a species changes so much that it is no longer sexually compatible with the original species from which it evolved, we can be sure that speciation has occurred: That is, a new species has arisen. The classic example often used to illustrate the phenomenon of speciation are the finches observed by Charles Darwin on the Galápagos Islands. I'm sure many of you have already heard of them. As part of his voyage of exploration around the world, Darwin arrived in the Galápagos on September 15, 1835, aboard the brig HMS *Beagle* and remained there for five weeks. His surveys of the flora and fauna of the archipelago during that brief period of exploration are certainly to be remembered as among the most important in the history of science. The Galápagos are an archipelago made up of eighteen major islands and many smaller ones characterized by numerous endemic species (living only on those islands) that were fundamental for the elaboration of the theory of evolution. On these islands, Darwin observed many species which, although similar, were undoubtedly different, each from the others, due to small but indisputable differences. This is the case of giant tortoises, whose carapaces differed slightly depending on the island on which they lived, and of Darwin's finches. These, although they were all quite similar both in size and plumage, were distinguished from each other by the shape of the beak, which had developed in response to the type of feeding. Darwin's formidable idea was that all of these different species of finches were derived from a common ancestor. We now know with certainty that the common ancestor of these finches colonized the Galápagos around two million years ago, and then evolved into eighteen distinct species that today are very different in body size, beak shape, song, and feeding habits. And Darwin's intuition about their origin was perfected when, in 2015, a study published in *Nature* clarified that the differences between these species were due to small differences in the ALX1 gene, a gene that regulates skull development in humans and other vertebrates and leads to differences in beak shape in finches.[9]

But let's read a passage from *On the Origin of Species* that makes clear to us, without the need for any further

ORNITHOLOGY.

1. Geospiza magnirostris.
3. Geospiza parvula.

2. Geospiza fortis.
4. Certhidea olivacea.

From September 15 to October 20, 1835, Charles Darwin explored the Galápagos Islands and described its flora and fauna. This is one of the decisive moments in the development of his theory of evolution. In particular, the many species of finches that populated the various islands of the archipelago and which had different-size beaks, adapted to different diets, seem to Darwin to be a very clear case in which several species differ from a common ancestor. Today we know this phenomenon as adaptive radiation.

comment, the depth of Darwin's intuition in an age, it is well to remember, in which the conviction of science was that species had been created independently of each other by an act of divine will.

The most striking and important fact for us in regard to the inhabitants of islands, is their affinity to those of the nearest mainland, without being actually the same species. Numerous instances could be given of this law. I will give only one, that of the Galapagos Archipelago, situated under the equator, between 500 and 600 miles from the shores of South America. Here almost every product of the land and water bears the unmistakeable stamp of the American continent. There are twenty-six land birds, and twenty-one, or, perhaps, twenty-three, of these are ranked as distinct species, and are supposed to have been created here; yet the close affinity of most of these birds to American species in every character, in their habits, gestures, and tones of voice, was manifest. So it is with the other animals, and with nearly all the plants, as shown by Dr. Hooker in his admirable memoir on the Flora of this archipelago. The naturalist, looking at the inhabitants of these volcanic islands in the Pacific, distant several hundred miles from the continent, yet feels that he is standing on American land. Why should this be so? Why should the species which are supposed to have been created in the Galapagos Archipelago, and nowhere else, bear so plain a stamp of affinity to those created in America? There is nothing in the conditions of life, in the geological nature of the islands, in their height or climate, or in the proportions in which the several classes are associated together, which resembles closely the conditions of the South American coast: in fact, there is a considerable dissimilarity in all these respects. On the other hand, there is a considerable degree of resemblance in the volcanic nature of the soil, in climate, height, and size of the islands, between the Galapagos and Cape de Verde Archipelagoes: but what an entire and absolute difference in their inhabitants! The inhabitants of the Cape de Verde Islands are related to those of Africa, like those of the Galapagos to America. I believe this grand fact can receive no sort of explanation on the ordinary view of independent creation; whereas on the view here maintained, it is obvious that the Galapagos Islands would be likely to receive colonists, whether by occasional means of transport or by formerly continuous land, from America; and the Cape de Verde Islands from Africa; and that such colonists would be liable to modification;—the principle of inheritance still betraying their original birthplace.[10]

In short, thanks to the Galápagos and the finches that had differentiated from each other on those islands to the point of forming new species, Darwin had been able to imagine the way in which new species were born. But the emergence of a new species, while perfectly comprehensible in theory, is very difficult to observe in common practice. Mind you, this is not to say that Darwin's theory is not supported by scientific evidence; there is literally plenty of it, including the formation of new species. The point lies in the difficulty of observing a phenomenon, evolution, the effects of which require many generations before they become apparent. This is where cities come into play: They are the perfect place for the creation of new species through a particular process called *allopatric speciation*—a complicated name with a meaning that is actually very simple. Imagine that geographic barriers were separating a portion of a population of individuals belonging to the same species. For example, imagine that a river separates a portion of a population of nonswimming, nonflying organisms from the rest of the individuals of the same species. For them, the physical barrier of the river will be impassable. Now imagine that this isolated population (these new territories are called, not by chance, islands) continues to live, always in this condition of isolation, for a sufficiently large number of generations. What will happen is that the different environmental conditions will produce, over time, a series of genetic changes, so that isolated individuals will no longer be able to interbreed with the original population. In practice, a new species will have been produced.

The presence of this type of insurmountable barrier, sometimes created by natural events, now occurs with increasing frequency due to human activities, especially those related to urbanization, which divide or interrupt habitats in which animal or plant species previously lived, giving rise to phenomena that in the long term can lead to the creation of new species. Take, for example, what is happening to rats in New York. In 2018, a group of ecologists from Fordham University, on analyzing the genomes of 262 rats, discovered that these animals were developing different genetic profiles depending on different neighborhoods,[11] and that the same thing was happening in other cities such as New Orleans, Salvador in Brazil, and Vancouver in Canada.[12] The explanation was to be found precisely in that allopatric speciation of which we were speaking. Architectural barriers, roads, or canals divided rat populations, inducing genetic variations linked to different areas of the same city. As in the case of water fleas or subway mosquitoes, which differ according to the different underground lines, these genetic modifications found in rats of the species *Rattus norvegicus* should be considered as the first signs of a process that over time (a long time) could lead to the emergence of new species. Other adaptations that are changing rats in the city are their skulls, which are slowly transforming so that they have longer noses and shorter teeth. Similar modifications seem to be common in all rodents living in cities and could be, it is hypothesized, considered as adaptive toward a diet made up of human food scraps.

All the animal species that share the environment of our cities with us, therefore, are in some way changing their behaviors. Cities pose several problems for the species that decide to live in them, the resolution of which often requires significant modifications. Think, for example, of how difficult it can be for birds to settle into such a different environment. Many birds, in order to be heard despite the background noise typical of the city, have raised the pitch and volume of their calls; in response to the city's continuous illumination, they have changed their circadian

rhythms; and, finally, they have accelerated the nesting period due to the increase in temperature. Although these
changes are mostly adaptive and have nothing to do with
genetic modifications, over time it is not impossible to
imagine, for most of the species that share the urban ecosystem with us, the generation of a series of urban counterparts. The same is true for plants, as we shall see.

PLANTS

The city has the capacity to change definitively the animal
species that populate it, to the point of giving rise to au-
thentically new species, different from those from which
they originated. I mention this so that you may always be
clear about the potency of the action of urban environments on life.

If animals are subject to such evolutionary pressure, it
is to be expected that plants, which for obvious reasons
are even more tied to the environment they inhabit and
more dependent on it, are also more sensitive to such pressure. And, indeed, plants in the city are undergoing such
dramatic and rapid changes that in every species exam-
ined so far, adaptive, or evolutionary, changes are so important that even pointing out the main characteristics
alone would require a long time. What is striking is that
research carried out on plants is a very negligible fraction
compared to that carried out on animals. Yet, every time
we have looked at plants, the results have been extraordinary: Plants are changing their mechanisms of action,

their defense strategies, and, in general, their behaviors to adapt as best as possible to urban ecosystems. In addition, plants are essential to ensure a chance of survival for our cities in the coming years. Studying if and how they adapt to city environments should be a priority of science, not a subject of research for a few original and extravagant researchers interested in secondary subjects such as botany. Are plants changing their behaviors to adapt to the urban environment? Are they able to do it? And to what extent and at what speed? These are just some of the questions that would be essential to answer immediately before trying to imagine any sustainability strategy for our cities. For example, are plants changing their diffusion mechanisms?

To answer this question, in 2008 Pierre-Olivier Cheptou of the CNRS of Montpellier began to study a very common plant in the city, where it usually occupies small plots on the sidewalks, in small residual areas or around trees: the *Crepis sancta*.[13] This seedling, whose common name is holy hawksbeard and which belongs to the Asteraceae family, is common throughout the Mediterranean, where it occupies disturbed habitats—cities. *Crepis sancta* has a peculiarity concerning its seeds that makes it very interesting for studying the effects of the urban environment on the dispersion tactics of species.

The *Crepis* produces two types of fruit (achenes, to be precise): one rather large and heavy, without a pappus (those feathery, light appendages that favor the dispersion of the seeds by the action of the wind), and which tends to

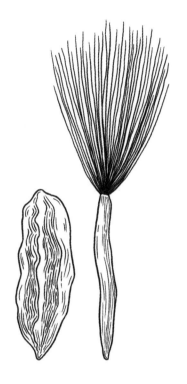

Holy hawksbeard (*Crepis sancta*) is a plant of the Asteraceae family, very common within the disturbed territories of cities. One of the salient characteristics of this species is the production of two types of fruits (achenes): a rather heavy one without a pappus or plume (on the left) that falls immediately next to the mother plant, and another that is lighter and equipped with a pappus (on the right) that can be carried by the wind.

fall directly to the ground, and another, on the contrary very light, equipped with a pappus, which can be carried by the wind for long distances. The fact that this plant grows in marginal areas of the city and that it has two types of fruit, equipped with different dispersal mechanisms, makes it a good model for studying what happens to seed dispersal in an urban environment. This is a matter of some importance, as the typical vectors of seed distribution—be they wind or water or different animal species—have a very different incidence in the city than in rural environments.

Think, for example, of all those species that entrust the possibility of spreading their species to the wind. They are many and are very common in urban habitats. But in the city, due to the frequent presence of very tall buildings or other architectural barriers, the wind velocity, if there is any wind at all, is much lower than in nonurban open environments. In fact, the lack of wind is one of the causes that leads to the formation of urban heat islands, which is why cities are so much warmer than the surrounding rural environments. And then, without wind, how can a species that entrusts the dispersion of its seeds to this very medium be able to thrive in the city?

We owe to Cheptou and his studies on the behavior of *Crepis sancta* some initial interesting findings on the subject. The researcher noticed that the populations of urban plants studied in Montpellier had a higher proportion of heavy fruits than that normally produced by this species in rural environments. To be precise, the amount of heavy fruit increased, as we will see shortly, from 10 to 14 percent. It seems like a small difference, but it represents a first decisive step of the plant toward a seed dispersion strategy more suitable for the urban environment. I will try to be clearer: In the dispersion of seeds, the strategies used by plant species can be different. There are species that produce huge quantities of seeds, relying on the wind or water to disperse them, and others that use animals as more reliable vectors. In this case, the seeds can be ingested, because they are contained in fruits that are appetizing to the animals, or they can use other particular strategies such as attaching themselves with hooks, adhesives, or other devices to the fur of the animals, as hitchhiker seeds do, obtaining in both cases to be transported around the world. Whatever strategy is adopted, what matters most is that the mother plant spreads as many seeds as possible far away from itself. In fact, if the seeds all fell close to the mother plant, we would have no diffusion of the species and, in addition, the offspring that were to develop next to the mother would find themselves competing with the other siblings and with the mother herself for a limited amount of space and nutrients. A situation that is far from ideal. The reason why *Crepis sancta* and many other species produce two types of fruit—one with diffusion mechanisms, another unable to travel and, inevitably, destined to fall close to the mother plant and remain there—depends on a kind of insurance policy for the future that some species like our *Crepis* put in place. This is why the percentage of fruit that is unfit for travel is normally small, around 10 percent. Similar to the strategy of a careful investor, who always places a portion of his savings in safe but low-yielding investments, as a safe haven in case others fail, in the same way, our *Crepis* also increases the quota of heavy seeds to ensure an active offspring in an environment such as that of the city, without wind, with high temperatures, and where the probability of a seed ending up in an inhospitable environment is very high.

To determine whether what was observed in Montpellier was a simple adaptation or rather the consequence of a mutation, the French researchers collected seeds from the city and others from the surrounding rural environment, planted them in a greenhouse under equal conditions, waited for the plants to grow, and collected their seeds. They recorded 14 percent of heavy achenes for urban plants compared to only 10 percent of the same achenes in rural plants. Using a mathematical model, Cheptou and his colleagues determined that the mutation had occurred in just ten generations. An incredibly short time.

So things are all right, then? Plants are equipped to deal with the urban challenge in the best possible way? Unfortunately, no. Whenever there are variations like those of *Crepis*, what actually happens is that the genetic isolation of these populations increases, with the risk that these plants will not be able to adapt quickly to new climate changes. Imagine, for example, that this change in the distribution strategy continues to affect the vast majority of achenes: What would happen if the environment were to change in some of its fundamental parameters? If for some reason (for example, a sudden pollution of the soil) the areas of Montpellier where *Crepis* grows were no longer favorable, the lack of light fruit would prevent the species from reaching new fertile areas where it could survive. In short, Cheptou's study has shown a great flexibility in the response of this species to the environment, which, however, could also jeopardize its future. This is the charm and curse of evolution: There is no right answer or ideal model. It proceeds by trial and error, each time selecting what is most suitable for responding to changes in the environment and sweeping away everything else. Let us always remember, in any case, that the fault would never be attributable to evolution but to our human upheavals, so energetic, sudden, and fast that they are not compatible with the proper functioning of evolution.

In 2017, a study was published which showed that genetic isolation, with the consequent loss of genetic diversity, is one of the general challenges faced by populations living in cities.[14] The study also found that one of its most frequent causes is linked to the *founder effect*, a fundamental concept of population genetics on which it is worth spending a few words. First described in detail by Ernst Mayr in 1954,[15] the founder effect is the process of the loss of genetic variation that occurs when a new population settles in a new place, starting with a very small number of individuals belonging to a larger population. A classic example is whenever a small group of migrants, not genetically representative of their population of origin, settles in a new area. These new populations show increased susceptibility to genetic drift, increased inbreeding, and relatively low genetic variation. In other words, the individuals that make up these populations are very similar to each other and, consequently, lack sufficiently varied genetic equipment to permit them to respond effectively to eventual environmental modifications.

A classic example of how this effect works can be found on those islands created from scratch by volcanic eruptions or where eruptions are so violent as to make a clean slate of preexisting life. Once the lava has cooled, a colonization process begins in which the effect of the founding populations becomes fundamental. This is what happened following the catastrophic eruption of Krakatoa in 1883[16] or on Surtsey island in Iceland, whose importance for studies on the colonization of barren lands I have already recounted in a previous book.[17] On both occasions, some of the first colonizing beings are plants, which settle in these new environments and create the conditions for a subsequent colonization by animals. But what interests us now is that the effect of the founder of these first migrating plant populations on the new territories is perfectly visible and measurable. Even for *Crepis sancta* populations that begin to produce heavier achenes within the small run-down urban areas they inhabit, the founder effect becomes critical. The plants within which the mutations originate are the founders of new populations that colonize restricted and, above all, isolated areas—that is, they are not in contact with neighboring areas. What happens on the islands, in a way, is no different from what happens in the city. It may seem strange, but the urban environment, because of its great fragmentation, is very similar for the purposes of evolution to an archipelago that is made up of thousands of small or very small urban islands (think of a flower bed or a small neighborhood garden) separated from each other by roads, buildings, barriers of various kinds that prevent mutual contact and the flow of individuals. Under these conditions, the sedentary populations typical of these urban islands tend to diverge from their initial populations in a short time. This is what happened to Darwin's finches in the Galápagos archipelago or to the *Crepis sancta*, water fleas, and brown rats in the jigsaw-puzzle archipelagos of urban islands that are our cities.

One of the most exciting studies of the effects of urbanization on the evolution of species concerned a plant that is widespread in almost every city on the planet, the white clover (*Trifolium repens*), and one of its special characteristics: the capacity to produce hydrogen cyanide both as a defense against predators and to resist in periods of drought. To investigate the effects of urbanization on this species, which is widespread in Tokyo as well as in London, Rome, Johannesburg, and Santiago, a global consortium was created in 2014, the Global Urban Evolution Project, consisting of hundreds of researchers from every continent. The aim of this global organization was to answer three questions: Does urbanization create similar environments in geographically distant cities? Do these similar environments cause clover to evolve along a common line, that is, do they show parallel evolution, in this case regarding cyanide production? And if so, what are the environmental factors driving this parallel evolution?

Analysis of results from a hundred and sixty cities across the globe showed that all white clover grown within cities produced less hydrogen cyanide than those grown in rural environments, either around or outside the city. A result that, all in all, is nothing more than a confirmation: It was

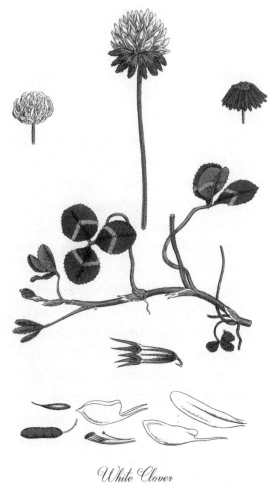

White Clover

TRIFOLIUM REPENS

White clover (*Trifolium repens*) is a plant native to Europe, North Africa, and western Asia that has been introduced as a grazing species everywhere. White clover is also one of the most common species in our cities, and as such is studied in many globally active trials that require collaboration between scientists and often also ordinary citizens (citizen science).

predictable that the lower presence of herbivores in the city would lead clover to reduce the concentrations of hydrogen cyanide, as had already been measured in other situations in the past. Whether this is to be called parallel evolution or, perhaps more properly, parallel adaptation is still too early to say. What is very striking is that the amount of hydrogen cyanide produced by plants in cities as diverse as Tokyo, London, Freehold in the United States, or Temuco in Chile was more similar than it was to that produced by clover grown in a rural environment.

This result is the demonstration of a fundamental truth: The distinctive characteristics of cities, wherever they are geographically located, whatever their history or current appearance, resemble each other more than they do the rural environments that surround them. Or, in other words, Florence and Johannesburg are much more akin to each other than Florence is to the countryside that surrounds it. It is a further and very convincing confirmation of the fact that our cities are ecosystems and as such are akin to each other, just as tropical forests or deserts resemble each other regardless of the region in which they are located.

The fact that these urban ecosystems are growing rapidly, and are potentially very difficult for most living species, should give us pause. So far we have only talked about the effects that the urban environment has on individual species, animal or plant, but the influence of cities is much deeper and more pervasive, because it acts directly on the set of relationships that unite the species of an ecosystem.

To clarify this question, one could examine an infinity of trophic chains—that is, the sequences of relationships between living beings that feed on each other—or of relations between living organisms. It seems to me that in this case, as in any other case in which it can be done, we should return to Darwin and his research. More precisely, the famous Galápagos finches that we have already mentioned. It happens that even in those remote and distant islands urbanization is advancing and population growth, the expansion of human settlements, and the motorization of island mobility are modifying the internal balances that had made this archipelago a paradise of biodiversity. The same goes for finches and one of their most traditional foods, the seeds of *Tribulus cistoides*, a perennial herbaceous plant that grows in arid plains and coastal habitats and is frequently found along roads, trails, and beaches, both in cities and in natural habitats of the Galápagos Islands.

This species produces fruits that are divided into five sections called *mericarps*. Each mericarp is defended by some sharp thorns that act both as a defense against predation and as a mode of seed dispersal. Finally, each mericarp contains one to seven seeds that can be accessed by opening the mericarp itself, a difficult feat for all but the larger billed of Darwin's finches. Now, with the advance of urbanization, finches, which had evolved different species capable of eating different foods such as seeds, nectars, or flowers, are quickly adapting to eating human food scraps, reducing the consumption of *Tribulus* seeds and thus limiting the spread of the species in rural environments. The *Tribulus*, meanwhile, is spreading more and more within urban environments, thanks to the fruits that stick to the bottom of shoes, tires, or various fabrics.[18] At the same time, populations of city finches, which are increasingly numerous compared to those outside the city, show a preference for the smallest and least resistant mericarps among those produced by *Tribulus cistoides* plants, thus influencing the size of future populations.[19]

It is really very difficult to predict how growing urbanization will affect the lives of the species that inhabit our cities. Will Darwin's finches change their diet again and therefore their beaks? And will *Tribulus cistoides*, which was mostly dispersed by these birds, find in other vectors, perhaps humans, an alternative means of spreading? It is impossible to answer these questions. There are so many relationships that bind living beings within an ecosystem, and there are so many alterations to the environment imposed by humans, that trying to imagine what will happen in a few thousand years (a laughably short time for evolutionary processes) is only a simple exercise in fantasy. We can't know; that's the truth. But we do know some important things: that studying and understanding evolution in urban environments is crucial, for example; that facilitating the maintenance of increased genetic diversity leads to greater species diversity at multiple trophic levels and promotes resistance to invasive species and increased primary productivity. These are all notions that we should use to create cities that are more resilient to environmental changes, by using management and design practices that aim to foster the persistence of populations and their expansion. To do this, urban planners and administrators would need to understand the fundamental function of evolutionary biology in the city. Will this ever happen? At the moment, predicting this seems more difficult than predicting what will happen to Darwin's finches.

HUMANS

We have always thought that evolution was such a slow process that we would never be able to observe the results of the life of living things in the short space of time of our urban history. And yet, here they are: Fish, birds, grasses, trees, insects, clover, and finches change their behavior and appearance at an astonishing speed, under the effect of the evolutionary forces produced by our cities. In practice, every living being that has been taken into consideration, with only a few exceptions, shows adaptations or real changes in the urban environment that in some cases have proved so significant as to lead to the origin of new species. All this in the space of relatively few generations. In light of what we have seen in others, it would seem legitimate to expect the same adaptive changes within our species as well. After all, we are the living beings that have lived the longest in cities and with a very large percentage of our total population.

There are many who do not seem to agree with this statement. There are many scholars who, in various ways, believe in our emancipation from the necessity of evolution.

According to them, the progress of our species has made us exempt from the effects of natural selection, and human evolution is now in our hands, no longer the survival of the fittest. What's more—and this is the most common argument—if almost everyone reaches old age, how can there be survival of the fittest? Human evolution is over, and from now on, thanks to advances in molecular biology, we will act on our own to improve those characteristics of ours that seem to us to require intervention.

It is a position influenced by the absurd idea that we have liberated ourselves from nature, that we are outside of nature and, of course, above it. This is yet another product of the human hubris that underlies so many of our catastrophic ideas. The reality is different:

Humankind is perfectly within natural processes and evolution will act on us with the same force with which it acts on any other living species. Not only are we subject to the laws of evolution, but if we think about the effects that the urban environment is exerting on our species, we are so in a clear and visible manner. More than any other living being, man suffers from the numerous selective pressures associated with urbanization, which modifies mortality, demography, disease transmission, air, water and soil pollution, hygiene, nutrition, social relationships, our microbiota, and dozens of other factors, each of which is fundamental in influencing evolution.

What, then, is happening to our species in the urban environment and what adaptations have already affected it is a matter of great interest.

As I have already mentioned in this chapter, today about 55 percent of the human population lives in cities.[20] Yet we do not have an exact perception of the magnitude and speed of this phenomenon. Meanwhile, cities cover only 2.7 percent of the planet's land surface, if the Antarctic continent is excluded from the calculation;[21] and on this tiny fraction of the planet, on which more than 4 billion people now live, 7 billion (70 percent of the population) will live there in 2070. It is an unstoppable phenomenon, and a sudden one at that. In fact, for most of the history of our species, that is, for about 290,000 years, we lived as nomads, hunter-gatherers, without permanent settlements. Then, around 12,000 years ago, with the agricultural revolution, we became farmers and, having to wait for the growth of crops, we became a sedentary species.

It is with the agricultural revolution, therefore, that our first permanent settlements, our first cities, and, with them, human civilization were born. Yet for much of the 12,000 years since that time, the number of people who have lived in cities has been limited to an insignificant fraction of the whole of humanity. Uruk, one of the first major cities in southern Iraq, probably had a population of some 50,000 at the time of its heyday, around 2000 BC, and was the largest metropolis of the time. The first city to reach a million inhabitants was Rome 2,000 years ago. Since then, numerous cities have passed on the scepter of the most populous city on the planet: Istanbul, Baghdad, many Chinese cities, London at the end of the nineteenth century

(6 million inhabitants), the New York metropolitan area at the beginning of the twentieth century (10 million), Tokyo (30 million in 1985). The Pearl River Delta, located in the Guangdong Province in China, is probably already today, or will become in a few years, the most densely urbanized region in the world with an estimated population of about 50 to 60 million people (the same population as Italy).

It is the speed of the phenomenon, as I have said, that is surprising, its exponential growth, like so many other curves that describe modernity. For most of history, humans have lived in low-density rural environments. Before 1600, it is estimated that the share of the world's population living in urban settings did not reach 5 percent. By 1800 this share had risen to 7 percent, and by 1900 it had risen to 16 percent.[22] Today, we are at around 55 percent and are moving rapidly toward a world in which humans will live almost exclusively in urban environments. It is a sudden revolution generated by the enormous number of advantages that living in the city entails, but whose consequences for our species are not yet at all clear.

Until a few years ago—not centuries or millennia—one of the distinctive characteristics of the human species was the ability to colonize any environment on the planet, even the most hostile and inhospitable. Apart from tiny portions that were decidedly inhabitable, in the space of relatively few years man had managed to expand, in practice, into every corner, even the most remote, of the Earth. Then, from the beginning of the twentieth century to the present day, our ability to live anywhere has suddenly disappeared, in favor of an unprecedented concentration of the great majority of individuals of our species within cities. It is such an enormous change in our behavior that it is quite impossible not to have equally enormous consequences on our evolution. In the meantime, no longer living on the entire surface of the planet but having grouped ourselves into tiny areas characterized by unique and common features, the human species seems to have lost the characteristics of a generalist species and assumed those of a specialist species. The difference is huge, and the consequences can also be huge.

A generalist species is a species that can thrive in every environment, in a wide variety of conditions, using very different types of resources. A specialist species, on the other hand, needs stable and specific environmental conditions. Most species are not totally specialist or generalist, but are in intermediate situations, closer to or farther from the two extremes, while only a few are highly specialist or highly generalist. Among the first we find, for example, monophagous organisms, which can only feed on a particular type of food. Koalas that feed only on eucalyptus or pandas that consume bamboo are classic specialist herbivores; they can only feed on these foods. At the other end of the scale we have the more perfectly generalist species, such as omnivores that can feed on foods of a very different nature. However, specialization does not consist only in being able or not to eat particular foods but in the ability to live in different environments.

Think, for example, of the halophyte plant species. As their name suggests (from *hals*, salt; and *phyton*, plant), these plants are ecologically and physiologically specialized to live in saline soils. They are typically found by the sea, around brackish ponds, or in any other place with high salt concentrations in the soil. These plants can live in environments that are completely prohibitive for most other species. Within their confined environment, halophytes are extremely efficient, while outside of it, very often, they are unable to survive. Or think of cacti, which have specialized to live in environments characterized by very high temperatures and water scarcity. When it is within its environment, a specialist species has an advantage over other species; but when, for some reason, conditions change and specialization loses its advantage, these species tend to become extinct much more rapidly than generalists.

Another fundamental characteristic of general species is that their geographical distribution is very wide. It is clear that if a species can survive almost everywhere and in very different conditions, it has a greater chance of expanding than those whose range is limited to specific environments. Humans have always been a shining example of a generalist species: Omnivorous, able to adapt to environments as diverse as deserts, tropical jungles, or perennial ice caps—in the course of their short history as a species they have colonized every corner of the planet, expanding their range and adapting magnificently to every condition.

This was true at least until a few years ago, when the vast majority of human beings were still spread over the entire planet. As late as 1970, 70 percent of the human population lived fairly evenly distributed in rural areas of the planet. But today, with more than 50 percent of humanity living in cities and with this percentage expected to rise to 70 percent by 2070, does it still make sense to describe ourselves as a generalist species? It should be remembered that already today in Italy 72 percent of the population lives in cities, and that this share in France, Spain, and Great Britain is well over 80 percent, as is the case in the entire American continent. In short, we are witnessing a revolution in human behavior comparable only to the moment when hunter-gatherers became farmers. Living in cities, humanity has embarked on a new path, one typical of a specialist species.

I do not think this is an exaggeration. When the vast majority of a species lives in an environment as peculiar as the urban one, characterized, as we have seen, by high temperatures, lack of vegetation, impermeability of the soil, air pollution, population density, and dozens of other equally important factors, and when, within this same environment, it behaves far more effectively than happens elsewhere, then I believe that the close interaction between the urban environment and the ability of our species to thrive can only be described as that of a specialist species. Being aware of this becomes essential to protecting ourselves from the dangers inherent in this specialization. As already mentioned, a specialist species thrives within its ecological niche as long as environmental conditions remain stable, but when these vary for some reason, the outlook becomes less rosy. Today, for example, after a long period of uniform climate, we have been witnessing in a handful of years its complete upheaval due to global warming. What consequences will it have on a species that is increasingly linked to a particular and fragile environment such as the urban one?

These are questions that are difficult to answer today, but that we should start asking ourselves. Human beings no longer have much in common with what they were up until a few centuries ago. Today we have become something different: We are urban people and the fact that this upheaval has taken place in so few years, and above all is affecting many billions of individuals and not our few sparse ancestors of the agricultural revolution, suggests that a wonderful laboratory of human evolution on a global scale is about to inaugurate its activity. We cannot predict what the results will be, but human evolution appears destined to take a path traced by the evolutionary pressure of cities.

It is worth pointing out that *Homo sapiens* has been evolving into an urban species not since yesterday but since agriculture was invented. Our genomes have already been transformed by what gave birth to cities, that is, agriculture, and they continue to transform at a great speed. Think, for example, of the anatomical mutations induced by the change in diet that took place with the agricultural revolution. The dentition of people ten thousand years ago was much more robust than today's, with the individual teeth around 10 percent larger. Since we started eating softer foods that require less chewing, in generation after generation not only our teeth but also our jaws have shrunk.[23] And not only the difference in texture but also the difference in terms of nutrients has triggered mutations: Think of what it has involved to change our diet toward one based on cereals and rich in starch. In a short time, thanks to agriculture and the cultivation of cereals, many human populations found at their disposal large quantities of excellent, very energetic foods, easily preserved, but which they did not digest at their best. In order to be able to do so, to have this new and extraordinary source of energy fully available, it was necessary to wait (not for long, actually) for evolution to modify in humans the efficiency of one of the tools that make it possible to assimilate starch: the enzyme alpha-amylase.

Alpha-amylase is the enzyme that catalyzes the breakdown of starch into sugar by breaking down the glycosidic bonds of polysaccharides to produce maltose, which can be hydrolyzed into glucose and absorbed into the bloodstream. All vertebrates produce this digestive enzyme in the pancreas, but only a few mammals, including humans, have evolved to produce alpha-amylase in their mouths, where it is secreted by the parotid and/or submaxillary glands. Almost every human being today has several copies of the AMY1 gene responsible for the production of amylase, and

their number is related to the level of salivary amylase produced (the greater the number of copies, the greater the
amount of salivary amylase). Producing many copies of the
same gene is one of the simplest ways to increase the production of a particular protein such as alpha-amylase. So
today, compared to a chimpanzee that has only two copies
of the AMY1 gene, a European or descendant of Europeans has fifteen. Individuals from populations whose diets
have traditionally included large amounts of starch tend to
have multiple copies of salivary amylase. Thus, the Japanese have more copies of the amylase gene than the Yakuts,
who are genetically close to the Japanese but whose diet is
predominantly based on fish. Similar differences have also
been found between Tanzania's predominantly carnivo-
rous Datog tribes and the Hadza, hunter-gatherers who
consume large quantities of tubers and roots.[24] This ability
has evolved as a direct consequence of the radically changed
diet in favor of foods with a higher starch content, consequent to the invention of agriculture. In starch-rich diets,
having many copies of the AMY1 gene means producing a
lot of salivary amylase and this, in turn, allows a greater
ability to digest this molecule, transforming it into easily
absorbed glucose. Without a doubt, this was a great evolutionary advantage for individuals who lived in an environment where resources were limited.

But today? For our contemporaries, does having all
these copies of AMY1 continue to be an evolutionary advantage? Most modern human populations living in urban

settings are certainly not limited by the amount of food resources available. On the contrary, one of the biggest problems in many urban areas of the planet seems to be linked to overeating that leads to an increase in the levels of obesity and type 2 diabetes. In this new context, the increased availability of glucose following starch consumption due to higher levels of salivary amylase could be considered a disadvantage. Should we expect a reduction in amylase activity in the future because of the huge availability of food in urban settings? It is one of the most likely adaptations to the urban environment. Given the relative speed with which we have been able to equip ourselves with tools to digest starch more efficiently, one would expect that we will also be able to limit its absorption in the event of excess. A bit like the birch moth did: from white to black and back. But the evolution of a species like man, in which there are many factors that act on evolution, is even more difficult to predict than what happens with other species. In fact, there is no way to know in advance what will happen. We can be sure that evolution will continue to work on us, but we cannot imagine the solutions.

Another thing we can be sure of is that the quality and the quantity of food we consume has a great influence on our evolution: Drastic changes in the diet of our species can also change our genetics. This has happened with cereals, as we have seen, but also with milk.

All mammals suckle their offspring, and it follows that every mammal in its infancy, including humans, can digest the components of milk, especially lactose, which is the main carbohydrate in milk. To digest lactose, you need an enzyme called lactase, which can break down lactose into two simple sugars: glucose and galactose. In most mammals, lactase activity is dramatically reduced immediately after weaning. For many human populations, however, its persistence, which is the result of recent evolution, makes it possible to digest milk or dairy products even after childhood. What is surprising about this recent evolution of humans is the time at which this ability developed. A recent study reveals that the persistence of lactase would have developed only around five thousand years ago, that is, four to five thousand years after the start of cattle breeding by humans.[25] In other words, for millennia humans consumed milk without being able to digest lactose, and this happened because the related ailments—diarrhea, flatulence, and stomach pain—are not such as to compromise life in any way. Then, due to some extreme event such as famine or severe epidemics, those who were able to digest milk were favored and passed on this ability to their descendants. Today, lactase persistence is present in 80 percent of the European population and its descendants, while it is very low in Africa and in large parts of Asia, and almost nonexistent in Bantu and in much of the Chinese population.[26]

Why the digestion of lactose is considered to be a beneficial adaptation is a more complex issue and numerous hypotheses have been put forward. Among these, one of the most accepted concerns the link between calcium, UV light, and vitamin D_2.[27] Exposure to ultraviolet light is essential for mammals to synthesize vitamin D, which in turn is necessary to ensure proper absorption of calcium, an essential factor for bone growth and health. Since the amount of UV light is low at high latitudes, there will be a limited synthesis of vitamin D and a consequent low absorption of calcium. For the populations of northern Europe, the possibility of consuming milk, which contains both vitamin D and calcium, would have been a fundamental advantage. The fact that lactase persists in almost all northern Europeans seems to confirm its adaptive advantage, especially at these latitudes.

The ability to digest starch and milk, which has enabled our species to expand its nutritional capacity enormously, has had a fundamental influence on our evolution. We have become what we are today thanks in large part to these small evolutionary adaptations so recent in our history. And it is fascinating to note that both of these adaptations are the offspring of human-made revolutions. Thanks to agriculture and pastoralism, we have begun to produce new foods, and thanks to evolution we have modified our genome so that we can fully use them. These are only the first steps toward a new urban species, on which the selective thrust offered by today's urban revolution will act with an irresistible force, greater than that exercised in its time by the agricultural revolution.

One of the key characteristics of cities is their high population density, a density never reached before in the history of our species and whose consequences must not be underestimated. Today, a population that until a few centuries ago was spread over enormously larger territories lives in an area of a few square kilometers. Take, for example, the case of Japan: In 1800 the entire population of Japan was 30 million. Today, that number of people is found within the Tokyo metropolitan area alone. Examining the data on the population density of cities, we realize that the world record belongs to Malé, the capital of the Maldives, with a density of 79,000 people per square kilometer, followed by Manila with 43,000 people per square kilometer and many cities in India. The first European city, in tenth place in the ranking of the most densely populated cities on the planet, is Levallois-Perret, a suburb of Paris that has a population density of 27,000 people per square kilometer. Never in the history of our species have so many lived so close together. And this is, in essence, the reason for the revolution that has brought us all to live in the city: to be in close proximity. Proximity induces efficiency in almost any sector you want to consider, be it commercial, industrial, cultural, social, or of any other nature. Being numerous means multiplying the possibilities and sharing the costs.

All true except there are some other considerations, not secondary, that concern our health. In fact, although health care, in particular care provided by hospitals and specialized services, is more readily available in cities, and the research that allows us to fight diseases is produced in research centers, laboratories, and universities concentrated in urban areas, the ease and very high number of contacts typical of cities has always represented a clear risk of spreading epidemics. In addition, the proximity not only to many other people but also to a large number of animals that share the urban space with us—the synanthropic fauna—facilitates the emergence and spread of epidemics. Many synanthropic species not only carry pathogens capable of infecting humans but also are reservoir hosts for these same pathogens. In addition to rodents, birds, bats, and insects, animals that are found in cities all over the world and normally act as hosts for zoonoses (diseases caused by agents transmitted directly or indirectly from animals to humans) include some mammals such as the fox in Europe[28] or the raccoon in the United States.[29] The reemergence of important zoonoses such as plague, leptospirosis, or hantavirus infection, all pathogens carried by rodents, is directly linked to the increase in urbanization in many developing countries. In short, the places with high population density have always been preferred for the production of new zoonoses, for the conservation of old zoonoses, and for their diffusion.

> He knew what those jubilant crowds did not know but could have learned in books: that the plague bacillus never dies or disappears for good; that it can lie dormant for years and years in furniture and linen chests; that it bides its time in bedrooms, cellars, trunks, and bookshelves; and that perhaps the day would come

when, for the bane and the enlightening of men, it would rouse up its rats again and send them forth to die in a happy city.[30]

It is enough to reread Thucydides, Lucretius, Boccaccio, Defoe, Manzoni, or Camus, as in the famous passage from *The Plague* given above, to relive the tragedies caused by the epidemics that have irregularly accompanied human history and understand how the rare possibilities of salvation lay only in fleeing from the cities. This is the reason why, since the nineteenth century, medicine has been so concerned with investigating the relationship between high population density and the onset of epidemic diseases. From well before the plague of Athens in 430 BC to the Covid outbreak of the present day, cities have been the place where infectious diseases have found the ideal conditions to spread.

Given this long custom, it might be expected that populations with a substantial history of urban settlements would have developed disease resistance to a greater extent than those without urban habits. This is what seems to have happened in the case of tuberculosis, probably the deadliest scourge ever to strike humankind, capable of causing a billion deaths in the last two hundred years alone and, even today, there are more than ten million new cases every year.[31] Approximately a third of the world's population is a carrier of the tuberculosis bacillus and is at risk of developing an active disease.[32]

The tuberculosis bacillus (*Mycobacterium tuberculosis*) seems to be inextricably linked to our recent revolutions. It belongs to an unusual family of bacteria that has infected various animals and birds throughout its history and, according to classical theory, passed to man at the same time as the origin of animal breeding. In this sense, the genetic analogy between *Mycobacterium bovis* and *Mycobacterium tuberculosis*, so similar that they can be considered practically the same species, does not seem to leave room for doubt that tuberculosis is the first of a long series of pathogens systematically introduced into our species as a result of our proximity to the animals we raise. In any case, whatever its origin, what interests us now is that tuberculosis has become humanity's deadliest killer since we started living in cities and that these millennia of coexistence may have induced in us forms of adaptation. This is according to research in 2011, which shows that inhabitants of areas with a long history of urban settlements are more likely to possess a particular protective genetic variant that provides resistance to infection.[33] Working on DNA samples from seventeen human populations in Europe, Asia, and Africa, and comparing their resistance rates to diseases such as tuberculosis or leprosy with their urban history, the study purported to show that prolonged exposure to pathogens in cities resulted in widespread disease resistance among these populations, which our ancestors then passed on to their descendants. The results show that the protective variant is found in a large part of the population, from the

Middle East to India and in some regions of Europe, where cities have existed for thousands of years.

Cities are, therefore, a fundamental selective force in our resistance to disease. The high population density that characterizes life in the city, and which is such an important factor in shaping so many aspects of our species, affects not only the way in which diseases spread but also all our adaptations to resist them. However, the urban environment does not just cause deaths due to epidemics. In fact, judging by the data, deaths from infectious diseases appear to represent only a small fraction of the deaths associated with the urban environment. Certainly, a fraction of the deaths from pollution.

Every year, according to a study published in *The Lancet*, 9 million people die prematurely from pollution.[34] Air pollution, mostly caused by combustion vehicles, remains responsible for the largest number of deaths, at around 6.7 million people. Water pollution is responsible for 1.4 million deaths, and so on. This is a statistic that, as the study states, despite the impressive number is only a very partial estimate of what really happens. For many substances, we have no idea how many deaths they can cause, even though we know for sure that they have large impacts on human health. And we're not talking about low-use chemicals. We do not have, for example, reliable estimates of deaths linked to pesticides, asbestos, mercurial, chromium, and a huge number of other chemical compounds that are not covered by the *Lancet* analysis. So this is a very incomplete figure.

Other studies give even more alarming data. Harvard research reveals that 8 million people die each year from fine particulate matter (PM2.5) alone, caused by burning fossil fuels.[35] This would mean that the total number of deaths from pollution is even higher. In any case, even if there were only 9 million annual deaths due to pollution, we are talking about 1 in every 6 deaths on the planet. And almost all of them are related to the urban environment. A fact that we will talk about again, and which by itself makes it clear what enormous selective pressure the urban environment exerts on human beings, as well as on every other living being.

In short, living in the city, despite its enormous advantages, also involves risks. Furthermore, to be precise, the dangers of city life, consisting mostly of childhood diseases or epidemics, have for centuries led to a negative demographic balance for cities. More people were dying in the city than were being born. In 1650, for example, London needed 6,000 new citizens every year to maintain its population. A century later, in 1750, the mortality of the city of London alone was such as to wipe out half of the population growth of the whole of England.[36] Since man created the first urban settlements and for many millennia, cities have acted as a brake on population growth. Until the twentieth century, mortality rates were generally higher in urban areas than in rural areas, a phenomenon known in English as *urban penalty*. Among the causes of this higher mortality, in addition to epidemic diseases, it must be considered that before the twentieth century most cities did not have adequate facilities for the disposal of waste generated by the high densities of humans and animals, and that there were neither prevention techniques nor treatment possibilities for gastrointestinal diseases associated with these living conditions. It was not until the beginning of the twentieth century that life expectancy in cities began to be higher than in rural areas. However, today as in the past, waste and pollution could in a very short time tip the scales of survival in favor of the country. *The Lancet* again informs us that, since 2000, deaths caused by modern forms of pollution have increased by 66 percent due to industrialization, uncontrolled urbanization, population growth, and the combustion of fossil fuels.[37]

What will happen to our species due to exposure of a large part of the population to such a difficult and toxic urban environment is one of the many questions that we cannot answer. We can, however, be sure that the selective pressure of the city will act on us as on other species, modifying and adapting our characteristics to an environment that is so new and different from what humanity has ever experienced before.

Five

URBAN METABOLISM

If the best way to understand a city is to study it as if it were a living being that is born, develops, dies, and is subject to the laws of evolution, then to understand how it works it is essential to analyze its metabolism. Through the study of urban metabolism, the similarity between a city and a living being suddenly becomes clearer and more rigorous. In addition, thinking in terms of urban metabolism opens up access to a series of well-validated and robust techniques typical of biological studies, which, once transferred to the field of urban studies, provides a new and rich perspective on the city.

But first it is worth spending a few words to dispel any doubts about what is meant by this term. The word *metabolism* (from the Greek *metabole*, "change") refers to the set of chemical reactions that make life possible. Its three main functions are the conversion of the energy contained in food into energy available for cellular processes; the conversion of food into building blocks such as proteins, carbohydrates, fats, etc.; and the elimination of metabolic waste.

In the process of carrying out these functions, metabolic reactions can be referred to as *catabolic* when they involve the breakdown of compounds and *anabolic* when they concern the construction (synthesis) of compounds. In the first case, in catabolic reactions, energy is usually released, while in anabolic reactions, that is, the synthesis of new compounds, energy is usually consumed. The combination of these reactions allows living beings to grow, to maintain their structures, and to respond to their environments.

The first to attempt to measure the metabolism of a living being was made by Sanctorius of Padua, a great Italian physician active at the turn of the sixteenth and seventeenth centuries at the University of Padua. To measure the fluctuations of body weight and, above all, to measure the amount of matter that disappeared on its way through the body, Sanctorius built a mobile platform connected to a scale on which the subject under examination could carry out some daily activities. In this way, it was possible to measure changes in body weight by taking into account the weight of the meals ingested and the weight of the solid and liquid excretions. His *De Statica Medicina* of 1614 was the first systematic study of basal metabolic rate.

Analogous to Sanctorious's approach, the idea of studying the city by considering the entry and exit of energy and material flows dates to at least the second half of the nineteenth century. More precisely, it was the idea of Patrick Geddes, the brilliant urban botanist we met a few pages ago. Geddes, let us remember, lived at a time when the

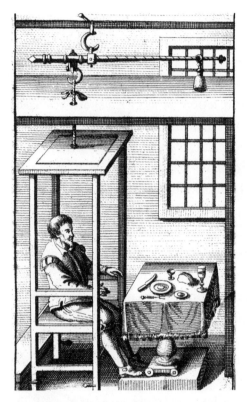

Sanctorius of Padua, the founder of modern experimental physiology, was the first scholar to understand the need to quantify phenomena in medicine. To obtain quantitative parameters, he devised many instruments that are still in use in medical practice today, such as the clinical graduated thermometer. He was also the first to devise an instrument (represented in this engraving that appears in his *De Statica Medicina*) to measure human metabolism.

prevailing sentiment was a belief in unlimited industrial progress. Thus, his ecological critique of limitless urbanization, which Geddes demonstrated to be physically impossible with his studies of the metabolism of the city, remained completely unheeded at the time, just as it remains largely ignored today.

According to Geddes, the functioning of cities was based on factors that could be measured quite precisely. To calculate them, in 1885 he measured energy and material flows by reporting them in a table that recorded every entrance into and every exit out of the urban system.[1] The table consisted of a list of the energy sources and materials needed for each product used in the city. For more detail, the consumption of materials and energy was divided into three phases that concerned the moment in the production cycle at which these materials and energy were used. The table, which was very detailed for the times, also included intermediate products used for the manufacture or transport of the final products and the calculation of energy losses. What was clear, from these early pioneering attempts by Geddes, was that the resulting final product, in quantitative terms, was often surprisingly scarce compared to the total material inputs that had been required to produce it. In other words, Geddes realized that the metabolism of cities, as opposed to the actual metabolism of any living organism, is incredibly inefficient. The difference is that the flows of energy and materials in a city are mostly linear: They come into the city and go out, leaving behind huge quantities of waste that are dumped on the street. Real biological processes, however, are always cyclical, that is, they have evolved in such a way that every tiny fraction of the energy and incoming materials is used, without any waste.

It thus becomes clear, from Geddes's first measurements, that due to this reduced metabolic efficiency, the impact of a city on the environment cannot be sustained for long. The city requires enormous flows of energy and materials that must come from outside, and produces equally enormous amounts of waste, in the form of solid waste, wastewater, and air pollution.

If one compares the efficiency of a plant's metabolism with that of a city's metabolism, one realizes that using the same term sounds almost blasphemous. The metabolism of a city is much closer to that of an animal than to that of a plant. Plants are autotrophic organisms, meaning that they can elaborate the organic substances necessary for the construction and functioning of the organism starting exclusively from inorganic (mineral) compounds and with the sole intervention of the light energy of the sun absorbed by chlorophyll. On the contrary, animals, heterotrophic organisms, being compelled to take organic substances already elaborated by other organisms to construct the organic substances of their own bodies, can only live saprophytically, that is, at the expense of dead organisms, or parasitically, at the expense of living organisms.

The city, therefore, built following only the criterion of animal organization, is like a botched experiment, a monster that is part saprophyte, part parasite. Like an animal, it consumes unlimited amounts of resources and accumulates mountains of partially consumed waste around it, like those creatures of science fiction who claim countless victims to survive and whose burrows are nothing more than heaps of uneaten or poorly digested remains. In fact, due to their inefficient metabolism and endless appetite, procuring all the resources they consume and purifying the amount of waste that our cities produce requires surface areas that are orders of magnitude larger than those occupied by the city itself. Imagine a spider standing still in the center of its web: We could thus represent the city at the center of the region on which its survival depends. A canvas the size of a soccer field, of which the city occupies only the midfield circle. Or, to give a concrete example, the canvas around a city like Rome would have the dimensions of that part of Italy that goes from Emilia-Romagna downward, including Sicily and Sardinia.

This measurement of the surface area necessary for a city like Rome to survive is called an *ecological footprint*, and it is a very useful tool for measuring the impact of a city on the environment. The inventors of this measure, Mathis Wackernagel and William Rees, describe it as "an accounting tool that makes it possible to estimate the resource consumption and waste processing needs of a defined human population or economy, in terms of a corresponding production area."[2] It is to all intents and purposes a measure of area, quantified in hectares, which takes into account the extent of land necessary to produce all the resources (food, water, fuel, materials, etc.) used by the inhabitants of a city and to purify their waste. Thus, this measure can refer to a single person, a society, a city, or an entire nation. There are more or less detailed methods for measuring the ecological footprint of cities, and surprising results are obtained from their application.

For example, returning to the case of Rome, its ecological footprint is estimated at around 20 million hectares.[3]

I know from direct experience with my students that surface measurements are not so immediately visualizable,
especially those expressed in hectares, acres, etc. As long
as it is a question of imagining surfaces of 1,000 to 10,000
square feet, we don't have any problem; these are extensions with which we are familiar. But when we start talking
about acres, thousands of acres, millions of acres, or even
square miles, we normally have no idea how big they can
be. So to understand the extent of the ecological footprint
of a city like Rome, let's consider that to reach 50 million
acres (equivalent to 78,125 square miles) we have to put together the extension of the entire south of Italy (Abruzzo,
Molise, Campania, Puglia, Basilicata, and Calabria, equal
to 28,271 square miles), Sicily and Sardinia (9,830 square
miles and 9,194 square miles, respectively), central Italy
(Tuscany, Marche, Umbria, and Lazio, 22,414 square miles),
and Emilia-Romagna (8,691 square miles). Well, now we
have a clear idea of the surface area needed for a city like
Rome to survive. And if we want to understand what such
an extraordinary extension depends on, we must study the
contribution of the various categories of consumption. Still
with respect to Rome: In first place we have food which ac-
counts for 27 percent, in second place transportation (25
percent), then consumer goods (clothing, electronics, cars,
books, and anything else you can think of) which account
for about 15 percent, accommodations around 8 percent,
services (5 percent), resources required by companies (14
percent), and the public sector (6 percent). That Rome alone

needs a large part of Italy's land area to continue functioning makes clear the main problem of cities: their unimagi-
nable appetite combined with the ridiculous inefficiency of
their metabolism.

If a city consumes so much to grow and develop, it is
necessary for those resources to be produced somewhere
else on the planet. The most obvious consequence of all this
is that, without a doubt, there is a limit to the size that cities can reach on the surface of the Earth. I mean, the fact
that cities occupy only 2 or 3 percent of the planet's habitable surface, while it may not seem like much, is probably
already beyond our planet's ability to accommodate them.
Their expansion is destined to stop due to the physical
limitations that prevent them from growing ad libitum, or
without restriction. There is no space on the planet to produce the resources needed to feed a larger urban area. For
cities to continue to extend their size and, above all, their
population, huge quantities of materials and energy are
needed that must be taken from somewhere on the planet
and transported to the city. This implies a predatory (and
thus typically animal) policy toward the planet's limited
resources.

We have seen that 27 percent of the ecological footprint
of a European capital like Rome is allocated to food. Food
is almost always the most important item in measuring a
city's ecological footprint. In lower-income cities, it is not
uncommon for food to account for around 50 percent of the
ecological footprint. What does this mean in terms of the

planet's consumption of resources? Or rather, in the light of this data, how much of the planet's surface is destined for food production? These are numbers that we should know in order to understand how our life in the city is directly connected to what happens on the rest of the planet, starting with the knowledge of how the surface is mainly used today. Excluding the areas covered by ice, which represent about 10 percent of the land above sea level, and the barren areas, that is, deserts, beaches, rocks, etc., which represent another 19 percent of the remaining area, 50 percent is used for agriculture. That seems, frankly, like a huge amount. Just to visualize what we are talking about, it is an area equal to five times the size of the United States. There is a tendency to think that the surface of land used for food production is not compressible: We will have to eat, and if this is the land we need, then there is not much we can do. In fact, if we look at how this gigantic expanse of land is used, we find that 77 percent of it is used to breed livestock and only 23 percent to produce plant foods.[4] This amounts to a system of land management so illogical that it is hard to think that an intelligent species is responsible for it; we reserve 77 percent of the land devoted to food production for animal husbandry, which produces only 18 percent of the calories destined for humanity! Is this really necessary? Is it sustainable, or even vaguely conceivable, for an intelligent species to use an area four times the size of the United States to produce 18 percent of its calories? Even the most convinced supporter of the consumption of animal products, I am sure, would find something to think about in these numbers. Especially because to recover all this land on which to raise animals, we have had to destroy most of our forests.

For almost all of the 300,000 years since *Homo sapiens* appeared, the Earth was a place covered in forests. It is estimated that, as recently as 1,000 years ago, only 4 percent of the nondesert land above sea level that was free of ice had been deforested to make room for fields cultivated for food production. Temperate forests, which still covered almost 990 million acres in the eighteenth century, have completely disappeared[5] and tropical forests are also in steep decline.[6] In practice, from 1700 to the present day, we have cut down 4,450,000,000 hectares (10,996,189,475 acres) of forest to make room for our needs; a little less than twice the surface area of the United States, to continue to use this unit of measurement. In just a few years—one thousandth of our time on Earth—we have reduced the space allocated to forests to a measly 37 percent of the inhabitable area, to make room for boundless agricultural land that, in reality, we would not need at all.

Therefore, to survive and grow, cities rely on ever-increasing resources whose origin we do not think too much about. Already today we would need 1.6 Earths to maintain the current standard of living, and in the future, it will continue to get worse. According to the World Bank, within twenty years, the median income class, that is, people earning between $275 and $2,750 a month, will grow from the current less than 2 billion to somewhere around 5 billion—3 billion more people, who by consuming meat, water, fuel, metals, and raw materials, will increase the consumption of the Earth's resources to levels much higher than today's already unsustainable consumption. At this rate of consumption of natural resources, asking how long it will take before the planet is no longer able to sustain our current civilization is not a rhetorical question but a very serious question to the study of which many people are dedicated.

In short, the ideas of planets transformed into cities such as the sci-fi planet-city of Trantor imagined by Isaac Asimov, as well as the dreams of some urban planners who imagine a widespread city capable of covering most of our planet, are unattainable fantasies. The reason lies precisely in the finite nature of the planet's resources and the inefficiency of the metabolism of cities. Karl Marx had already intuited this concept of inefficient metabolism from the first significant studies on the ecosystemic relationships between humans and their natural environment. In *Capital* he writes:

Capitalist production collects the population together in great centers and causes the urban population to achieve an ever-growing preponderance. This has two results. On the one hand it concentrates the historical motive power of society; on the other hand, it disturbs the metabolic interaction between man and the earth, i.e. it prevents the return to the soil of its constituent elements consumed by man in the form of food and clothing; hence it hinders the operation of the eternal natural condition for the lasting fertility of the soil.[7]

Moreover:

> On the other hand, large, landed property reduces the agricultural population to a constantly falling minimum, and confronts it with a constantly growing industrial population crowded together in large cities. It thereby creates conditions which cause an irreparable break in the coherence of social interchange prescribed by the natural laws of life. As a result, the vitality of the soil is squandered, and this prodigality is carried by commerce far beyond the borders of a particular state.[8]

This "irreparable break in the coherence of social interchange" could now be translated into an irreparable break of urban metabolism. The Earth's resources are squandered because they are imported into the cities and lost there because of the lack of that *return to the soil of its constituent elements consumed by man*. Precisely because of that inefficient metabolism that does not allow cities, as happens instead to every living being, to consume the minimum necessary by reutilizing most of the matter and energy used in other cycles. Or, to put it more simply, to recycle. As Jacob Moleschott, a Dutch physiologist and contemporary of Marx, who most likely inspired the German philosopher, wrote: "What man eliminates, nourishes the plant. The plant transforms air into solid elements and feeds the animal. Carnivores feed on herbivores, to become in turn prey to death and spread new life in the plant world. This exchange of matter has been given the name of organic replacement."[9] It is the same organic replacement of which Marx spoke and whose meaning has now expanded to the point of being identified with social metabolism: a very useful concept thanks to which we can extend the measurements concerning the metabolism of an individual to an entire society,[10] thus having a tool to understand, from an environmental perspective, how much room is still left on the planet for further growth of cities and their consumption.

The idea of being able to measure the social metabolism of a city has a long history. If we had to identify a starting point for studying the city as a machine that converts resources into waste, it would be with the 1965 publication of Abel Wolman's essay "The Metabolism of Cities."[11] It is in this article that we read that water enters urban metabolism and comes out as sewage, or iron enters as such and comes out as scrap. Wolman paves the way for an innumerable number of studies that quantify in detail the flows of water, materials, energy, and nutrients entering and leaving a growing number of metropolitan areas. The second fundamental theoretical contribution to the success of social metabolism comes from Herbert Girardet, who draws a distinction between circular and linear metabolism: the former characterizes the natural world—the waste of one organism is the sustenance of another—and the latter characterizes the urban world, where resources come in and are wasted.[12] The global environmental crisis, it follows, should be read as an excessive proliferation of linear metabolisms as cities grow and spread. For Girardet, urban metabolism includes everything that is needed to transform natural materials into the needs of our societies, or, in other words, "it is the conversion of nature into society."[13] A brilliant idea that encompasses any type of material or energy transformation that takes place within the city.

The question becomes more complex when we try to measure the metabolism of humanity. Or rather, it would not be so complex if we limited ourselves to measuring its biological metabolism, or in other words the amount of energy needed to ensure that all human beings can survive. An average person has a basal metabolic rate of around 80 W. This metabolism, which is the sum of all the energy expended on the main vital metabolic functions such as respiration, blood circulation, nervous system activity, etc., represents 45 to 75 percent of the total daily energy expenditure, which, for a human being, amounts to approximately 120 W, more or less the energy needed to operate an average-size LED television.[14] This is an amount of energy quite in line with that consumed by any other mammal of similar mass, with the difference that we humans allocate a share of basal metabolic rate of around 25 percent to the functioning of the brain, a percentage much higher than that allocated by other mammals to the same function. As a result, we have less energy to devote to other functions like growth and, in effect, compared to other mammals, we grow less. From this perspective, our growth resembles more the growth of a reptile than that of a mammal.[15]

Up to this point, the metabolism we have been talking about is biological metabolism. Humans, however, consume resources not only for their biological metabolism—indeed this proportion is quite insignificant—but also for all the rest of their activities: their social metabolism. When we try to calculate this overall metabolism (biological and social combined), the numbers change significantly in magnitude, depending on the stage of our history. A hunter-gatherer had a metabolism that could be estimated at 300 W, a farmer 2,000 W, while a contemporary of ours, after the industrial revolution, can have a metabolism ranging from 8,000 W for a Englishman to 12,000 W for an inhabitant of the United States.[16] An inhabitant of a rich country today has a metabolism between 70 and 100 times higher than their biological metabolism. At first glance, this might even seem like good news. During my classes, when I ask students to imagine the social metabolism of a modern European, I usually get hyperbolic figures that have no bearing on reality. These are almost always very exaggerated figures that arise from the widespread idea that our senseless impact on the planet is orders of magnitude greater than that of other living beings. When I tell them that, in fact, our social metabolism is only between 70 and 100 times higher than other mammals of the same size, the first reaction is one of disbelief. *Only* 100 times more? I can't believe it: In their instinctive assessments, our impact should be hundreds of thousands of times greater, not just 100. How else could the combined disaster be justified? Yet 100 times the energy consumption is really an enormity. It is perfectly adequate to describe the extent of our activity in preying on the planet's resources. Why doesn't this amount, 100 times, seem adequate to represent our impact?

A few years ago, in search of a system that would improve the perception of what it really means to have a metabolism 100 times higher than what our size would require, I read an illuminating essay written by Yadvinder Malhi in which he used an original system to visualize our impact on the planet: to make it visible in terms of body mass.[17] I will try to be clearer. Living beings other than humans do not have a social metabolism (or when it does exist it is completely irrelevant in terms of energy); their use of energy is necessary only to satisfy their biological metabolism. In 1932, Max Kleiber, a Swiss agricultural chemist at the University of California, Davis, was working on measurements of the energy metabolism of farm animals. While looking for a way to compare the nutritional needs of animals of different sizes, Kleiber found that raising an animal's body weight to 3/4 power obtained a reliable measure of its metabolism. Later it was realized that this relationship, which in the meantime had been given the name of Kleiber's law, had a general value and was a valid measure for all living beings, from bacteria to giant sequoias, from microorganisms to plants and animals.

To express it symbolically, Kleiber's law states that, if we call q the metabolic rate of the animal and M the mass of the animal, then $q \sim M3/4$. From such a law it follows that, as the mass of a living being increases, its metabolic consumption per unit mass is less. To understand what we are talking about, let's take a field mouse, which weighs an average of 30 grams (1.6 ounces), and a cat, whose average weight is 4.5 kilograms (10 pounds). If we apply Kleiber's law to the weights of these two animals, we realize that the cat's metabolism is only 43 times higher than that of the mouse, while its weight is 150 times greater. In other words, a larger living being consumes much less energy per unit mass. It seems that this reduction in energy is regulated by constraints due to the architecture and the transport network that limit the maximum metabolic rates in gradually larger organisms.

In any case, this is one story, just as another very interesting story is the fact that Kleiber's law can also be applied to the growth of cities.[18] What interests us now is that, just as it is possible to have a credible estimate of metabolism from the weight of an organism alone, it is also possible to obtain the inverse, that is, the weight of an organism whose metabolism is known. If we apply this inverse formula to the social metabolism of humans, the result is fascinating. A farmer of the preindustrial period with his 2,000 W of metabolism would have a mass of about 2.5 tons, about that of a rhinoceros, while a modern person of the industrial period with their 12,000 W (if static) of metabolism would have an estimated mass of about 15 tons. That's more than twice the size of an adult male elephant, the largest of the land mammals.

Now try to imagine a primate weighing 15 tons. It would look a lot like King Kong. And, continuing this effort of imagination, try to imagine the United States populated by 310 million King Kongs. By using King Kong as a unit of visualization of our impact on the environment, everything becomes clearer and even my most intransigent students are satisfied with the image that is obtained. It is inevitable that billions of King Kongs will have a major impact on the planet's metabolism. I live in Florence, a city of 370,000 residents and that hosts millions of tourists every year. To imagine it populated by this immense population of giant apes who every day convert linearly huge quantities of resources into waste is perhaps a rather extreme image, and it does not consider the many fantastic things that are produced in the city, but I think it is helpful in the difficult task of expressing exactly our impact as citizens on the environment.

We said that the vision of billions of King Kong devastators is only partially true. We have a lot in common with primates—after all, *Homo sapiens* is a primate—but if we think about the way we live in cities, the organisms we have most in common with are social insects. Our cities, from this point of view, should be studied as colonies of millions of individuals, as E. O. Wilson suggests, by introducing an analogy from which we could derive important information.[19]

So what happens when you apply metabolism studies to an ant (or termite) colony and a human city? For one thing, Kleiber's law is also valid for colonies of social insects, approximating the size of the colony to that of a single individual. What I mean is that if we calculate the metabolism of an ant colony using their total mass as if it were that of a super ant, we realize that Kleiber's law works perfectly, and as the colony increases, the energy consumption of its mass units (of each individual ant) decreases. In other words, in a larger colony each ant will be slower and so consume less energy than an ant in a smaller colony. The reason for this slowdown is probably due to the greater difficulty for each individual to find the necessary amount of food in a larger colony. In any case, this is not what interests us, but rather to know what happens in our cities as they grow in size. Will we also have a slowdown in the number of individuals who make it up? Of course not. As it is easy to imagine and to experience, the reality of our cities is often the opposite of what happens to large colonies of insects. In one research study, Luís Bettencourt analyzed a wide range of activity measurements within our cities and found that many of them function superlinearly (as the number of people increases, the number of activities per person increases).[20] From the speed at which people walk to the amount of their wages, from bank deposits to rates of invention, many things in the city increase in this way. But many activities remain linear (as the number of people increases, the number of activities per person does not change), such as the number of jobs, the number of houses, and the amount of water consumption. Still others, often linked to infrastructure, vary sublinearly (as the number of people increases, the number of activities per person decreases). Unlike social insects, the larger the cities in which humans live, the more active they are—due to greater opportunities, greater exchange of knowledge, and a thousand other benefits.

Bettencourt wrote that cities are like stars that burn brighter as they grow larger.[21] And, in fact, everything seems to happen faster in the city, from material and cultural production to innovation. Precisely because many of its parameters grow in a superlinear way, however, this furnace in full operation must find the resources to do so as well. If the sources of resources were always equal, such growth would lead to metabolic collapse. So where do these additional resources come from? Bettencourt suggests that they are born from innovation, the main place of production of which is the city. This is what prevents it from collapsing. Every innovation prevents the collapse of resources but, at the same time, also indicates the moment in the future when the next limitation will occur. In this way, cities would undergo phases of expansion and contraction of growth, as the cyclical trends that characterize the history of many cities would seem to testify. But how long will it be possible to compensate through innovation for the insatiable need for resources of these furnaces that are our cities? In the end, even the stars collapse, and there can be no innovation that goes against the laws of physics.

In the meantime, however, we can do everything in our power to limit the hunger of our cities and to transform their linear metabolism into a circular one. In this sense, I believe that an approach that is less focused on animal life and that considers the possibilities offered by plant organizations could turn out to be useful.

Six

THE DIFFUSE CITY

When compared to the life of the Earth, the human species in a mere handful of years has become a seismic force capable of changing history. The advance of our species and its activities over the past 10,000 years has changed the planet's energy metabolism with a force comparable only to the colonization of the Earth by plants. The results of this revolution are currently completely beyond our ability to predict. The truth is that, although even trivial common sense suggests avoiding excessive damage to our ecosystems, we do not know what to do to limit our impact on the planet without slowing down economic growth. Furthermore, our seeming incapacity to curb even the most insignificant consumption does not augur well for a happy future. In any case, nothing will be achieved without innovation, not only technological but above all social innovation. We need to innovate by imagining forms of global governance that can minimize the consumption of common goods before we approach critical thresholds. Once crossed, thresholds can no longer be recovered, certainly not without great sacrifices.

Devising a way to make this happen in both the social and technological spheres is the challenge of our future.

Whatever solutions we manage to invent, one thing we can be sure of is that for them to work, they must have a fundamental impact on the way our cities operate. Despite their occupying only a small portion of the Earth's surface, cities are the places of our aggression against the environment.

We saw in the previous chapter how the impact on the planet of each inhabitant of a rich Western city can be compared with, and above all visualized as, a 15-ton primate; a terrifying image, if multiplied by the number of wealthy city dwellers on the planet. But if we want to have a strictly quantitative idea of the impact of cities, descriptions are no longer enough, and we must turn to numbers. The data tells us that more than 70 percent of the world's energy consumption and 75 percent of the consumption of natural resources are attributable to cities. As is the emission of about 75 percent of carbon dioxide and the production of 70 percent of waste. A 2021 study of greenhouse gas emissions from 167 cities around the world showed that 25 megacities alone are responsible for 52 percent of these emissions.[1] Asian cities emit the most greenhouse gases, and most cities in developed countries produce significantly higher greenhouse gas emissions per capita than those in developing countries. Energy consumed by buildings of all types (residential, institutional, commercial, or industrial) contributes between 60 and 80 percent of total greenhouse gas emissions in North American and European cities, while in a third of cities more than 30 percent of total emissions come from road transportation. This data explains quite clearly who is responsible for global warming on the planet. If we think that within 25 years from now, cities will be called upon to host an additional 2.5 billion people, it is obvious that there is no imaginable serious solution to the problems related to our impact that does not include an urban revolution.

From this point of view, the challenge seems to be two-fold: While cities are the main source of our impact on the planet and the environmental changes that follow, they are also, and at the same time, the most vulnerable human habitat on which those same changes are acting. I will try to simplify the discussion by taking as an example global warming, the main and most dangerous of the human-made changes to our environment.

As I imagine everyone knows by now—I recall this here more out of duty than necessity—global warming is due to greenhouse gas emissions, the most important of which, in terms of the quantities produced by human activities, is carbon dioxide. As a result of the emissions of these gases, their concentration in the planet's atmosphere increases, preventing it from cooling. Thus, the average temperature is increasing at a speed never experienced before: We are already 1.5°C (2.7°F) higher than the temperature of the preindustrial period and forecasts for the end of the century tell us that the increase will be somewhere between 2°

and 3°C (3.6° to 5.4°F). There is no doubt about what causes this warming. What we still don't know with reasonable certainty is what its consequences will be for the planet and especially for cities, our new ecological niche, the place where well over 7 billion people will live by the end of the century. The reason for the uncertainty is that temperature influences every process that takes place on the planet, be it physical, chemical, biological, or ecological. So knowing what will happen, for example, to the planet's climate, atmospheric circulation, water cycle, sea and ice levels is very difficult to predict in the necessary detail.

Of one thing, however, we can be certain. The places where these changes will do the most damage are our cities. Many cities around the world are already facing the consequences of global warming, and things will only get worse in the future. The atmospheric phenomena that already cause excessive rainfall, fires, storms, and droughts will tend to increase their incidence, in terms of number and intensity, with direct consequences on the population and the economy of cities.

Think, for example, of the intensity and duration of heat waves, a phenomenon that has been revived in recent years with ever renewed vigor. Heat waves are periods characterized by extreme weather conditions during which very high temperatures are reached for several consecutive days, frequently associated with high humidity and lack of ventilation. The heat wave that hit the European continent during the summer of 2022 caused 61,672 people, mainly elderly and frail, to die from cardiovascular problems. A 2017 study estimates that even if we manage to limit the rise in average temperature by the end of the century to just 2°C (3.6°F) above the preindustrial level—a prospect that is now almost unattainable—the number of people in cities exposed to the effects of deadly heat waves would exceed 350 million.[2] Urban centers, in fact, are much warmer than the surrounding rural areas, as we saw earlier when we mentioned the phenomenon of heat islands.

We owe the discovery of the temperature difference between the country and the city to the London pharmacist Luke Howard. In 1820, he published *The Climate of London*, the first text to deal with the urban climate. After nine years of recording temperatures in central London and the surrounding countryside, Howard explains for the first time the phenomenon whereby the temperature of the city is higher than that of rural areas, and how this difference is greatest at night. Today, due to heat islands, it is estimated that, globally, the temperature in urban centers is on average 6.4°C (10.8°F) higher[3] (although this is a highly variable figure depending on geographical location of the city, its construction characteristics, and, above all, the extent and distribution of green areas).

That cities are so much warmer than their surroundings is mainly due to the artificial and impermeable nature of most urban surfaces. The lack of permeable soil prevents the evaporation of water and the consequent cooling of the environment. Many surfaces in the city are dark (think of asphalt and the like), thus absorbing a greater amount of solar radiation, and are made of materials that have unfavorable thermal properties. Moreover, a significant part of the energy used in cities by buildings, industry, or vehicular traffic is released in the form of waste heat, the geometry of buildings acts as a barrier to the passage of wind, and the radiant properties of the atmosphere are modified by pollution.[4] It is clear why cities are getting hotter. Now, if we add the effects of the urban heat island to the upheaval of the climate due to global warming, it becomes evident that cities, especially those located at unfavorable latitudes or altitudes, are already now and will become increasingly difficult places to live in the coming decades.

Having reliable models of how the urban climate will evolve in the coming decades will become essential if we want to try to imagine solutions. There are laboratories that are responsible for making simulations to predict what the climate of our cities will be like in the coming decades. First, it may be useful to know what the Urban Climate Change Research Network (UCCRN), a consortium of more than 1,200 researchers dedicated to the study of climate evolution in urban centers, writes on the subject. In 2018, the UCCRN published a report full of information that I will try to summarize in a few lines. To date, 350 cities on Earth experience extreme heat conditions, that is, periods of at least three months in which the average maximum temperature does not fall below 35°C (95°F). By 2050, there will be 970 of these cities. Today, 200 million people in cities live in extreme heat, rising to 1.6 billion by 2050. Today, 14 percent of the urban population lives in intense summer conditions, and in 2050 this share will rise to 45 percent.[5]

By 2050, over 650 million people living in more than 500 cities could experience a drop of at least 10 percent in freshwater availability; 2.5 billion people living in 1,600 cities could experience a drop of at least 10 percent in national yields of major crops; more than 800 million people living in 570 coastal towns will be at risk of flooding. Quite an impressive report to which the authors have given the appropriate title "The Future We Don't Want."

There are also a series of laboratories scattered among universities and research centers around the world that, using robust climate models, try to indicate what the climate of cities will be like over a time horizon usually limited to the next thirty years. The ETH Zurich does this through a simple but, I believe, effective system: For each city we choose, it indicates another that today has the climate most like that which the city in question will have in 2050.[6] We thus discover that in 2050, on average, cities will have the climates that cities located about 1,000 kilometers (621 miles) farther south have today. The climatic conditions of Rome in 2050 will be like those of present-day Izmir, London will have the climate that Barcelona has today, Paris that of Istanbul, and Madrid will be like Marrakech.[7] For those who are more interested in the fate of cities in the United States, the University of Maryland has set up a similar service which is limited to 540 American cities and with the more distant horizon of 2080. Again, there are no surprises: The climate of cities will become very similar to that of cities located about 800 kilometers (497 miles) farther south, with great changes not only in temperatures but also in rainfall and humidity.[8]

In short, in these past few years many universities have been inventing systems to disseminate with simplicity and impact what will happen to our cities. The aim is to make the climate future of our urban centers clear to as many people as possible. The results, despite their efforts, do not seem to be getting through, at least judging by the fact that the (large) majority of people continue to have no interest in—or are skeptical of—any topic related to global warming.

In any case, even if we can predict with a good margin of confidence what will happen to our cities in the next thirty or fifty years, the most important question remains: What can we do to make cities more resilient in the face of these now inevitable changes? And above all, what is being done? Let's start with this last question, which unfortunately is easier to answer.

In most cities, nothing is being done: People are behaving as if the phenomenon did not exist. In some cities, action plans are being prepared that almost always include early warning systems, changes of outdoor working hours, and, in some cases, the creation of cooling shelters that allow citizens to take a refreshing break. Finally, a few enlightened administrations are tackling the problem at its roots, trying to cool their cities as much as possible. These include the efforts of Seoul, which has planted 16 million trees to reduce its heat islands and particulate pollution to a minimum, and the attempt by European capitals such as Paris or Berlin to make their urban surface as permeable as possible, by replacing impermeable spaces with green spaces and disseminating solutions for greening roofs or building surfaces. These are all practices that make it possible to reduce the effect of heat islands and at the same time allow the city to adapt to the heavy rains that will increasingly characterize our future. In short, something practical can be done and quickly, you just have to want to do it. It is almost always a matter of simply planting as many trees as possible, making as much as possible of the city's surface area permeable. Yet how many cities are doing anything in this regard? Few. Almost all of them are limited to facade measures, whose real validity is inversely proportional to their media effectiveness.

That said, as with everything else about our strategies for responding to the environmental crisis, studying how other living beings are adapting could give us enlightening perspectives. So what are all the other inhabitants of our common home doing? How do species respond to the problems of global warming? If we had to give a blunt answer, it could be only: migration.

The history of the Earth, when observed over its long duration, has been a continuous succession of climatic, tectonic, and oceanic shifts, to which life has always responded through the ability of species to modify their distribution. Every species, be it animal, during its life, or vegetable, generation after generation, will tend to move from the most hostile places to those most suitable for survival. This is a general rule and there are no exceptions: When environmental conditions deteriorate, living animals migrate in search of better conditions. So let's see what's happening and if these migrations can also affect our species.

Let's start with marine species that are responding to rising ocean temperatures much more efficiently than terrestrial species (about ten times faster). For some decades now, more than 80 percent of marine species have been migrating to other places, changing their reproduction and feeding patterns. Some species have already migrated as far as about 1,000 kilometers (621 miles) from where they were abundant just a few decades ago.[9]

For terrestrial animals it's the same story: Bears, wolves, lynxes, squirrels, even the residual frogs and numerous species of insects are migrating in search of cooler climates. By studying more than 4,000 species distributed throughout the planet, it has been seen that about half of these are affected by migratory movements and move at an average of more than 15 kilometers (9 miles) per decade.

Pathogens also move with their vectors: Today malaria appears at an ever-increasing altitude, carried by mosquitoes onto the mountain slopes of places such as Ethiopia or Colombia, where living at a certain height has always meant being free from the scourge of malaria.[10] The same is happening with leishmaniasis, a sometimes-fatal disease, once predominantly tropical, which is moving north along with the sandflies that host the pathogenic parasite.[11] Furthermore, it's not just human pathogens that migrate; those affecting our crops migrate too.

These huge shifts of species have unpredictable outcomes. When one species migrates, so do all the others that depend on it. Thus, entire food chains can move—indeed they are doing so—with unprecedented consequences for our societies.[12] In fact, the redistribution of species, on both a regional and a global scale, affects the functioning of ecosystems, the production of natural resources necessary for food security, and a huge number of other fundamental processes such as the distribution of diseases or the processes of carbon dioxide absorption. Something we should start thinking about.

Even plants are not exempt from this mass flight to places more suitable for their survival. For decades, there have been studies regarding the northward or upward movement of the world's vegetation. In Spain, the populations of beech (*Fagus sylvatica*) and holm oak (*Quercus ilex*) are rapidly reaching higher and higher altitudes. The holm oak has reached the altitudes normally occupied by beech forests and the beech, in turn, has moved to heights that were prohibitive until recently.[13] In Scandinavia, populations of spruce (*Picea abies*) are now found at altitudes of up to 250 meters (820 feet) higher than in the 1970s, and birches (*Betula pendula*), of which until 1955 there was not

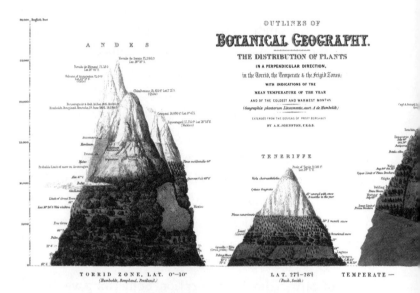

This illustration from an 1848 atlas inspired by the scientific discoveries of Alexander von Humboldt, the father of modern phytogeography, shows the altitude at which plants grow as a function of latitude and climate. In recent years, due to global warming, the maximum height at which different plant species live has been increasing more and more.

a single known specimen above 1,095 meters (3,600 feet) above sea level, now grow normally at altitudes of around 1,400 meters (4,600 feet) above sea level.[14] It is a phenomenon that anyone who lives in the mountains can witness.

If you look at the slopes of sufficiently high mountains from a distance, you will notice that there is a line that separates an area where trees grow from another above it, where the trees suddenly disappear, leaving room for

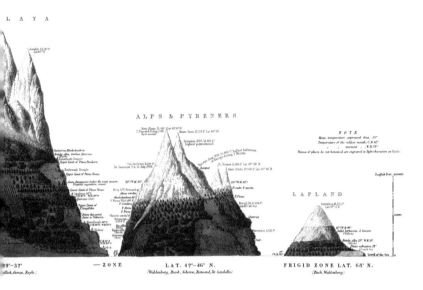

vegetation, usually only herbaceous. This very sharp line, called the *tree line*, indicates the level above which the environmental conditions no longer permit the growth of trees, often due to too low temperatures.[15] For years, because of warming temperatures, the tree line has been rising all over the planet: from Norway to Sicily, from Pakistan to Korea. Recently, a study using the analysis of satellite imagery considered almost 1 million kilometers (620,000 miles) of trees on 243 mountain ranges regularly distributed throughout the planet, whose altitude ranged from 489 meters (1,604 feet) on Khrebet Chayatyn in Khabarovsk, Russia, to 4,528 meters (14,855 feet) on the

Ruwenzori range in eastern equatorial Africa. From 2000 to 2010, 70 percent of the tree lines moved upward by an average of 1.2 meters (4 feet) per year. The fastest change was observed in the tropics, where the upward shift was about 3.1 meters (10 feet) per year, although there are strong differences related to different local characteristics. For example, in the mountains of Malawi, Papua New Guinea, and Indonesia, some tree lines are moving upward at a rate of 10 meters (33 feet) per year, while in other parts of the world, often due to the increasing number of fires, there are very modest retreats.[16]

In addition to altitude there have also been changes in latitude. Plants have been migrating northward at a rate that in some areas of the planet where global warming is hitting hardest, such as the Arctic, can exceed 50 meters (164 feet) per year, while on the rest of the planet the rate of northward migration seems to be a few meters per year. Whether it's 50 meters or 2 meters per year, for many species the speed of migration may not be sufficient to escape the consequences of global warming. This is not a trivial matter: If global warming were to change the environment at a rate faster than the possibilities of moving our forests, the consequences could be dramatic.

To address this risk, some of the world's most farsighted nations are setting up systems of assisted plant migration, thanks to which we will be able to move plant species to new areas in the hope that they will be able to colonize them.

One of the most obvious effects of global warming on plant life is the sudden and extraordinary displacement of

The Pedersen Glacier rises in the Kenai Fjords National Park in Alaska. These two photographs illustrate its state in the early twentieth century (above) and in 2005 (below). In less than a century, the glacier has retreated by 0.93 miles, leaving the field to diverse vegetation that also includes alders and spruces.

many agricultural crops northward carried out by humans. In just a few years, we are witnessing a subversion of the species cultivated in the different geographical areas. Until a few decades ago, for example, the northern limit of the range of the olive tree, one of the symbolic species of Mediterranean civilization, was thought to be the Apennines in Italy. To the north of Tuscany, the olive tree was found, albeit in small extensions, only in Liguria and around Lake Garda (two very particular microclimates). Today the olive tree is cultivated throughout Italy, up to the slopes of the Alps, well beyond that 45th parallel that for a long time had been considered its insurmountable limit.

Even more extraordinary is what is happening to the other symbolic plant of the Mediterranean: the grape. In recent years, its cultivation has increasingly moved north, and today there are vineyards producing commercial wine in Norway and Denmark. The big French producers are buying land to plant new vineyards between Normandy and Kent, betting on the reduction of the wine-growing area in traditional regions due to the impact of global warming and on the rise in temperatures in regions such as Normandy or Brittany, where the finest red wines have been produced for some years. The United Kingdom, famous for its beers, expects its vineyard area to double in the next ten years, fueled by demand for its sparkling wines. This northward movement does not seem to be slowing down. Even in southern Sweden, due to an increase in average temperature of about 2°C (3.6°F) in the last thirty years, there are already more than 200 hectares (494 acres) of productive vineyards which, according to many serious winemakers and enologists, will multiply their reach in the coming years.

Of course, it's not just Mediterranean crops that are migrating north; tropical plants are also subject to the same push. Southern Italy, Sicily, Spain's Andalusia, and other regions of southern Europe have become producers of mangoes, papayas, avocados, lychees, cherimoyas, and bananas of excellent quality that are also very popular with consumers. It remains to be seen what will happen to those tropical countries from which these plants come and where they were traditionally cultivated. On the one hand, they will find it increasingly difficult to cultivate due to global warming, and on the other hand, they will face competition from northern regions closer to the largest markets. This is just one more of the countless examples of how the troubles produced by the rich north of the world are unloaded on the inhabitants of the poorest countries.

Although agriculture is one of the key parts of many countries' economies, competition is not, unfortunately, the only or most important of the problems that global warming is creating in the world's hottest areas. More and more in the coming years, and already today, extreme temperatures and droughts do not or will not allow a good chunk of the planet to be habitable. There is no more painless way to put it: According to most models, in the next thirty to fifty years a significant percentage of the planet will be too hot to live in. This is not an apocalyptic prophecy but the finding of more and more research.[17]

Our species, like any species, has environmental limits within which it can survive. Despite our enormous technological advances, these limits still exist and cannot yet be overcome. Among these, the decisive one is the temperature range within which our survival is possible. For millennia, humans have enjoyed an average annual temperature of between 11° and 15°C (52° and 59°F). Within this average temperature range, we humans, along with our crops and livestock, have found ourselves in an optimal state for growth and development. This niche of time, which has allowed humanity to live comfortably for thousands of years without any significant variation, is changing at an unprecedented rate.

A recent study shows that with the current global warming scenario (that is, if we continue to do nothing), we will see such warming over the next fifty years that areas that are now home to around a third of the world's population will experience average annual temperatures above 29°C (84.2°F). These thermal values are currently present in only 0.8 percent of the earth's surface and are mainly concentrated in the Sahara.[18] At these temperature levels, in addition to being impossible to conduct any agricultural or livestock breeding activity, it is often literally impossible to survive.

To understand this point, we need to say a few words about a particular measure of temperature: the *wet-bulb temperature*. What's this about? It is a combined measurement of dry air temperature, as we would see it on a common thermometer, and humidity; together, these two parameters measure the danger of environmental conditions for human beings. The definition derives from the cooling effect of wrapping a damp cloth over the bulb of a thermometer and the consequent evaporation of the water in the cloth. This cooling depends on the humidity of the air. In fact, if the humidity of the air is very high (it means that the air is already saturated with water), then evaporation will be limited, and so will the consequent lower temperature. The higher the humidity, the closer the wet-bulb temperature will be to the dry-air temperature. The critical threshold for humans—the wet-bulb temperature to which a healthy person can be subjected for six hours before dying—is 35°C (95°F), which corresponds approximately to an air temperature of 40°C (104°F) in conditions of 75 percent humidity. Humans regulate their temperature through sweating, which, above that wet-bulb temperature limit of 35°C, no longer works, preventing us from cooling down. And when that happens, if we don't manage to cool ourselves artificially, the result is an increase in the temperature of the internal organs until they fail.

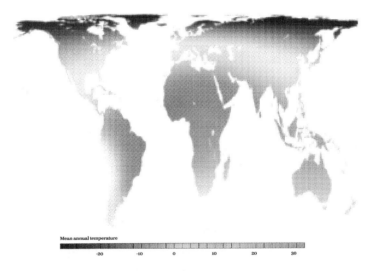

Mean annual temperature

-20   -10   0   10   20   30

If we were not to change our approach to global warming, by 2070 an average annual temperature of above 29°C (84°F) is expected to affect large parts of South America, Africa, the Middle East, India, and Oceania (indicated in dark red), whereas today this is the case only in small areas of the Sahara.

An important question is whether, and how many times, this limit has already been exceeded in some parts of the planet. In 2020, research reported that some coastal subtropical locations have already experienced a wet-bulb temperature of 35°C (95°F), even if only for a few hours.[19] This may sound like good news, but it is not: A great deal of previous research predicted that such rises over the limit temperature for human life would not occur for several decades. The same 2020 study revealed that, globally, the number of times a wet-bulb temperature of 30°C (86°F) was reached—still considered an event of extreme humidity and heat—more than doubled between 1979 and 2017. There have been about 1,000 cases of wet-bulb temperature of 31°C (88°F) and about a dozen cases above 35°C (95°F) in Pakistan, India, Saudi Arabia, Mexico, and Australia. In short, in many regions of the planet we have come close to a limit that will not allow them to be habitable. If we also consider that the limit of 35°C (95°F) of the wet-bulb temperature comes from a theoretical study and that, on the other hand, more empirical studies tend to lower this temperature to around a value of 31.5°C (88°F), it is clear that the scenario is even more worrisome.[20]

Since the regions potentially most affected will be among the poorest in the world, we can reasonably expect that large migratory masses from these areas will move north. Said in this way, it seems a simple enunciation of facts that are bound to take place, presumably, in the near future. In practice, such migrations will not be easily carried out. The

entire rich world is closing its borders even to today's ridiculously small numbers of migrants. What will happen
when *billions* of people move to survive? In a world that was,
let's say not ideal but only minimally rational, we would be
organizing ourselves now to manage an inevitable event.

I hope that we will show that we are an intelligent species, because this is going to be the century of great migrations, and imagining that we can prevent them is not a good
idea. Because it is not only animals and plants that need to
migrate in response to changes in the environment: For us
humans, too, the answer is to move. We are called animals
because we are animate, that is, we can move. To prevent an
animal (including humans) from migrating is to prevent it
from expressing its essence: the only way it knows how to
solve problems. Instead of preventing migration, we should
understand that migration is one of the most effective and
fastest responses to climate upheaval.

In addition, this unprecedented migration for the
human species will affect not only the people who live today
in the large areas of the planet that will soon become un-
livable but also the inhabitants of many rich cities on the
planet that will soon be unlivably hot. High temperatures
will affect everyone, rich and poor. Thus, in the next few
years, migrants will include not only a third of the population of Bangladesh, who now live along low-lying coasts
that will disappear under water, but also the inhabitants
of many rich regions who will migrate, partly because they
will be forced to and partly because they want to feel safer.

The Welsh villagers of Fairbourne, for example, will have to abandon their homes because there, as in Bangladesh, rising sea levels are submerging the coasts. They will be Britain's first climate migrants, and they won't be the only ones. The UK's national weather service tells us that sea levels across the country have risen by 15.4 centimeters (6 inches) since 1900 and, depending on future climate scenarios, could rise by up to 1 meter (3 feet, 3 inches) by 2100. Like Britain, many other places in the world will be affected by major migration events if sea levels really rise according to these forecasts.

And let us not forget the demographic phenomenon: Our planet's population will continue to grow, reaching about 10 billion people around 2060, but the greatest increase will occur in tropical regions, where global warming will push populations north. In the north, on the other hand, where hardly anyone is born anymore, an ever-increasing elderly population is supported by an ever-smaller workforce. Sooner or later (and the sooner the better) this economically and socially unsustainable condition will force Europe and the United States to do everything they can to attract migrants, not to reject them. Simple common sense. It will be a matter of going back a little in time to when states, in search of skills and taxes, were more committed to preventing people from leaving than to preventing them from coming.

If large numbers of people—entire populations—must migrate, many will be housed in existing cities, and other cities will have to be built, especially in the northernmost areas of the planet. The question is, how to build these new cities to be resistant. And, above all, how the cities that already exist can be transformed so that they can respond to such a challenge. How to cope with a future with so many variables? Living beings migrate by exploiting mobility to move from the source of the problem, and in a certain sense even the new cities—those that will inevitably arise farther north—could be considered as part of the same migratory phenomenon. But when it comes to existing cities, which cannot migrate, what are the lessons that, in this case, the observation of nature can give us? Or rather, what are the living beings that more than any other have shown that they can withstand changes in the environment without moving? I have no doubt that the only answer can be: trees. Only among trees can we find examples of resistance over millennia, and it is no coincidence that some of the world's most ancient but still-living cities and some of its oldest trees are of comparable age. In short, trees are the model that our cities should turn to for inspiration. So let's see what these characteristics are that make trees so long-lived and resistant, and try to understand if some of them could be adopted by our cities.

Seven

PHYTOPOLIS

In the southwestern corner of Sardinia, next to the small town of Villamassargia, there has been a magnificent olive grove for more than a millennium: S'Ortu Mannu, "the large vegetable garden" in Sardinian. I recommend a visit there to anyone who wants to understand what it means to resist as a tree. Although I had often heard of it, I had never had the opportunity to visit until a couple of years ago, when I was invited to give a lecture on plant resistance. It's hard to imagine a better place to talk about this topic. First, because S'Ortu Mannu is made up of centuries-old olive trees—some of which are certainly thousands of years old—whose very survival testifies to their ability to resist. Secondly, because in this monumental olive grove it is possible to observe closely one of the secrets that make the trees so resistant and long-lived: their modularity. We'll get to that in a bit.

The most impressive and famous specimen of the entire olive grove is an olive tree with a gigantic trunk of 16 meters (52 feet) in circumference. Her name is Sa Reina—the queen—and she's a miracle, a majestic tree with an immensely powerful and graceful bearing. Even without knowing her name, anyone who has even a shred of sensitivity to beauty cannot help but be awed by her royalty. Those who stand before Sa Reina see more than a thousand years of history become matter. The trunk is all twisted, folds in on itself, coils in chaotic confusion, without a clear trajectory. For those who are familiar with physics, I would say that it resembles the materialization of a strange attractor. For those who have no idea what the hell an attractor is, let

The modular architecture of trees and their diffuse organization, thanks to their ability to adapt to changes in the environment, make them extremely resilient living organisms. The olive tree in the photo is Sa Reina, "the queen" in Sardinian, a magnificent example of longevity and resistance that, along with numerous other olive trees, grows in S'Ortu Mannu, a park near Villamassargia.

alone a strange one, imagine a huge and twisted trunk, that's fine too.

Whether or not Sa Reina is the largest olive tree in the Mediterranean or one of the longest-lived is not important; the tree is huge and ancient, there is no doubt about that. But that's not what makes her great. What makes her unique is that she believes she is immortal. Or at least that's what I thought, looking at her. There is no animal that conveys the same idea of power. An elephant, a blue whale? Compared to Sa Reina, they have the effect of ephemeral little beings.

One of the most interesting features of Sa Reina and many of her centuries-old companions in S'Ortu Mannu is that, if you look carefully, you will see that the insides of their huge trunks often house large cavities that, in some cases, can take up most of their diameter. How is it possible, then, that these trees are still so healthy and vigorous? Just imagine if the same thing happened to one of those animals we were talking about earlier. An elephant that lost not most of its body, as happens to the olive trees of S'Ortu Mannu, but even only a very small fraction of it could not survive. For an animal, whatever its size, to die, all it takes is for one small fundamental organ to be removed or no longer function. A pound of flesh is enough. So what is the secret that makes these trees so long-lived? How do you live for millennia and remain as robust as the olive trees of S'Ortu Mannu? The secret is to be built in a modular way, without specialized single or double organs. The secret is to spread, rather than specialize. In a word: It is to be a plant and not an animal.

To understand better, we need to take a step back and understand the fundamental characteristic that distinguishes plants from animals. Movement! I'm sure this is the first difference that jumps out to everyone. Plants are stationary. It is the characteristic that strikes us most, even though it is neither true nor the most important. And yet, movement is the first thing that comes to mind: Moving is vital for us animals. We cannot imagine a form of life that does not have the ability to move. As we have said, for animals, moving is the answer to any problem. We can't even imagine that we can respond to any stress in the environment without moving. We are animated, endowed with movement, and that is why we are unable to imagine forms of life, let alone intelligence, that do not have the same characteristic. So powerful is the idea that movement equals life that anything that doesn't move isn't worthy of our attention.

Let's try to imagine an experiment. We find ourselves in an Italian piazza on a beautiful Saturday afternoon in spring. The piazza is crowded with a few hundred people enjoying the sun and chatting with each other. Suddenly, in the middle of the piazza, something materializes that we know with certainty comes from somewhere beyond the Earth (let's say that it has written on it the place it comes from). It is quite large, an ovoid and rough-hewn affair of about 1.5 meters (5 feet) in length. At first glance it is motionless. The appearance doesn't resemble anything we know, it's downright alien. Having no idea what it is, and especially whether or not it can be dangerous, we keep a safe distance from it, forming a perfect circle that has the mysterious thing at its center. Everyone feels entitled to have their say on what that globular affair is, and some opinions are so unlikely as to cause the crowd to laugh. Remember, we are in an Italian piazza on a beautiful spring Saturday afternoon, and thing or no thing, no one wants to miss the chance to relax and enjoy themselves.

For a while, everyone wonders what to do. The owner of the café calls the police. Then someone who does not want to miss the opportunity to demonstrate his courage in front of a lot of fellow citizens comes forward and after some hesitation, justified by the situation, driven to action by the shouts of encouragement of some and the brutal taunting of many others, proceeds and, stretching a leg to its maximum extension, touches the thing with the tip of his shoe. Nothing. The thing doesn't move. It's a good sign: It doesn't look dangerous. The brave man tries again, this time with more force and then again, repeatedly. Again, nothing: The thing doesn't move. It doesn't seem even to be alive, let alone intelligent. At this point, many others also come forward to experience the thrill of contact. Someone who is more methodical, and scientifically trained, closely examines the mysterious object in search of something that resembles, or even vaguely recalls, organs. They don't find anything, and that puts an end to the discussion: It's not something alive or intelligent. The scientists will take care of it. The police arrive and draw up a report against unknown persons for occupying public land.

If I have dwelt on a silly story, it is because the substance of this little digression is, after all, true: If a thing doesn't move and doesn't have recognizable organs, in our eyes it has no value because we can't assimilate it to ourselves. We can't understand it, in the exact same way that we can't understand plants. For us, they are an incomprehensible form of life because they lack the most distinctive ability of all: to move. In fact, as I have said, it is not even true that plants do not move. We should more correctly say that they do not move from the place where they were born, that they are rooted. In any case, leaving aside these small lexical issues, it is precisely from their inability to move from place to place, from their being rooted, that the extraordinary attributes of robustness that characterize their organization derive. It all depends on the fact that any living being unable to move has greater difficulty in defending itself from predation. It is for this reason that plants have evolved according to an organization that allows them to continue to live even if a significant part of their body is removed.

The trick of this resilient organization consists in the lack of single or double organs. Imagine if one of those olive trees of S'Ortu Mannu had been built as an animal with specialized single or double organs, therefore equipped with two lungs for breathing, a stomach for digesting, two eyes for seeing, a brain for reasoning, etc. The first microscopic damage, such as an insect-made hole in a key organ, would have been enough to kill it. To live millennia, no part of the body must be unique and irreplaceable, and for this to be possible, every fundamental function for life must be distributed over the entire body and not concentrated within specialized organs. Plant organization is exactly like that: diffuse and distributed, able to respond to catastrophic limitations without losing its ability to function. The exact opposite is true of animal organization, which is based on a rigid hierarchy and specialization where it only takes one of the organs to fail for the entire organization to collapse.

Indeed, an animal is built according to a hierarchical organization, which sees the brain, the head, rule over a series of single or double organs specialized in specific functions. It is the same model that we have reproduced in all our human organizations. You only have to look at any organizational chart to realize it. From the administration of a municipality to the management of a joint-stock company, from the hierarchies of any academy in any remote corner of the world to the management of a library, from the government of a nation to the administration of an apartment building, including, of course, the design and organization of our cities, the only scheme we are able to imagine is the one on which we ourselves are built: the animal model, hierarchical and specialized.

It's worth dwelling on why we're built the way we are. What are the advantages of this animal organization that we replicate everywhere? There is just one: speed. We are built to respond quickly to the demands of the environment. This is the only real advantage of a pyramidal and hierarchical model: Responses are decided by the boss and therefore executed in the shortest possible time. And no matter what the problem is, the response will always be the same: move. Moving from hot to cold, from places without food to those where food abounds, moving quickly to evade a predator or to catch prey. Different problems, one answer. If we want to be picky, we should say: different problems that we *do not solve* (because the problems remain) but we *avoid*, thanks to movement and decision-making speed. In this, we animals are truly unbeatable. It has taken hundreds of millions of years for evolution to perfect this ability of ours. A hierarchical organization, with a central command to which every decision is delegated, is the best thing you can have for speed to be displayed smoothly.

In the case of plants, responding quickly has no value. Faced with the problems generated by changes in the environment, a plant will have no choice but to solve them. Escaping is not an option. And since to formulate correct answers, you need to have as much correct data as possible about what is happening, a distributed, decentralized, literally rooted-to-the-ground organization proves to be the best you can hope for to accomplish this task. Coupled with the extraordinary sensitivity of plants, there is nothing better at dealing with the problems of stationariness.

In the light of these simple considerations, constructing cities according to an animal model designed for movement would not seem like a really good idea. Yet this is exactly what we have been doing for millennia: trying to assimilate our immobile cities to our mobile animal bodies, a reckless choice for which we are paying the consequences. On the contrary, the model to which the growth, development, and functioning of cities can be entrusted is, without a doubt, the plant model. Even cities cannot escape from problems but are condemned to having to solve them. Transforming our urban centers according to a plant-based model could, for example, make a fundamental contribution to resisting the climate crisis.

As we have seen, from at least the middle of the nineteenth century urban studies began to be inspired by the teachings and methods of biology. But what biology? Although key concepts such as metabolism or growth constraints apply to both plants and animals (with varying degrees of efficiency in the two kingdoms), it must be clear that the functioning of plants and animals is so different that it can be considered antithetical. Returning, then, to the question: What biology? The answer is without a doubt: the animal one. The teachings coming from the world of plants are so far unknown to urban planning.

Each of our cities, as we have seen, develops around a center that contains the functions of government while the rest of the territory is specialized in specific functions: the business quarter, sports centers, hospital zones, nightlife, university campuses, etc. It is impossible not to see in it the precise imprint of animal organization. Even though we have been talking for years about the multicentric city, the diffuse city, or more recently the fifteen-minute city—all concepts that seem to suggest a transition from the vertical organization of the animal kingdom to the horizontal organization that characterizes plants—in practice cities continue to be designed and built on the founding idea of concentration and specialization. In some cases, this concentration of functions can lead to decidedly extreme solutions.

Many years ago, I visited Tokyo for the first time. In spite of its gigantism, I tried to do what I have always done to get to know a city: walk around it as much as possible. Of course, walking all over Tokyo would require the perseverance of a true urban explorer. I met a professor there who, since the day of his retirement, had dedicated every morning to exploring the streets of the city, summer and winter, 365 days a year. At 7:30 in the morning, after breakfast, he would leave the house, take the subway to the area he wanted to explore, and visit the streets one by one, checking them off from the map as he went. At 12:30 he got back on the subway and returned home in time for lunch. In seven years, he had visited about a third of the city's streets and wondered if he would live to complete the entire exploration. Well, my approach was not nearly as maniacally systematic as the professor's. I simply tried to make the most of my little free time by taking the subway to the center of one of the thousand districts of Tokyo: Nakano, Asakusa, Ginza, Roppongi, Meguro, Tsukishima, Ikebukuro. Once I arrived in the middle of a neighborhood, I walked aimlessly through its streets.

One of my personal yardsticks for evaluating how much I like a city is the number of bookstores, parks, and trees I find along the streets. The more trees and bookstores I see, the more I think that city is a good place to live. This simple method for evaluating the quality of life in a city has never betrayed me. Except in Tokyo, where the system didn't seem to work. I had been visiting the different districts of the city for many days and I had never come across a bookstore. I wandered far and wide, slipping into side streets thinking that they could be hidden in more protected areas, but nothing. Wherever I looked, there was no sign of one; sometimes there would be a stationery shop or newsstand, but never a real bookshop. It was a very strange thing, since each of those districts had the population of an average European capital. How was it possible that there were no bookstores?

At first, this intolerable absence made me a little indisposed toward the city. There had to be something I didn't understand. I was so stubborn about finding a bookstore that in every neighborhood, after a fruitless search street by street, I began to ask anyone I could if they knew of any bookstores. The answers, however, due to the precarious language skills on both sides, seemed completely incoherent to me. Anyone I asked began with nonsensical ramblings that invariably ended with something that sounded to my ears like *bamboccio*, the Italian word for "chubby boy." It made me laugh a lot: What did they mean by *bamboccio*? I had expected someone to say to me: Look, go straight down this street and take the second right and you'll come to a bookshop. Instead, they all responded with incomprehensible explanations that ended with the continuous and obsessive repetition of *bamboccio, bamboccio.*

Now, I don't know if it happens to you that once a sound is associated with a meaning, it is very difficult for you to hear anything else. It happens to me a lot. So it took me a while to understand: They weren't saying *bamboccio* but Jimbocho. It was a neighborhood that specialized in bookstores. There I would have found as many as I wanted.

Indeed, Jimbocho is a book lover's dream. The promised land of every bibliophile. The subway stop is decorated with pictures of books; the cafés are full of people reading. Everywhere you see people laden with books going from one side of the street to the other. There are hundreds and hundreds of bookcases leaning against each other. In practice, most of Tokyo's bookstores are concentrated in the Jimbocho area. The fact that it is equidistant from as many as five major universities is one of the reasons for this strange concentration. The second is that the Japanese like to group some of a city's functions in specific areas. This aspect is so intrinsic to the hierarchical and specialized idea of Japanese cities, that even beauty is concentrated in specific areas. Japanese cities are not pretty. At least not in our Western conception. However, in almost every city there are magnificent areas where beauty is concentrated, where the parks, streets, temples, and houses are cared for with that dedication and attention to detail that we associate with Japan. For the Japanese, beauty is not something that has to be everywhere. Like everything else, it must be concentrated in some designated area of the city where specialization allows for superior results.

But is it really efficient that in order to visit a bookstore you have to go across the whole city? And that the same thing should have to be done to buy an electronic device or walk in a park? Is it a good thing that you have to go shopping in malls and that to get a blood test everyone has to go to the city's specialized health-care center? And, above all, is it a good thing that the population is grouped into different areas according to social class?

It's always the same old problem between animal and vegetable, concentration versus diffusion. On the positive side, in a specialized place, prices, services, competition, the possibility of comparing offers, or just the synergy between like-minded operators will offer a higher result on average. The negative side is less immediate to understand but, I am convinced, is of much greater absolute value: Specialized areas are constitutionally weak. This is a simple, basic notion of ecology, a subject that all those involved in the functioning of cities, in any capacity, should be obliged to know: Wherever biodiversity is reduced (even in different areas of a city), the risk of the environment becoming unstable is much higher.

How many industrial zones, shopping malls, business districts, entertainment centers, office complexes do you know of in your cities which have gone down the drain in the space of a few years and now represent black holes, dead spots, within the organism of the city? Often the reasons why entire specialized areas become necrotized are completely trivial, futile, or imponderable: changing tastes, improved techniques, the whims of the market. It takes nothing for an entire area of the city to be lost. If an urban area is not polyfunctional, it has no chance of surviving. If the reason for specialization disappears for whatever reason, the whole area no longer has a reason to exist. This drift of urban concentration has distant origins, but in recent years it has taken a paradoxical turn, with not only some areas of some cities but rather entire cities specializing in a single activity: for example, tourism, or technology, or sports.

How many cities of art-based tourism do we know in Italy, which only a few decades ago were magnificent living organisms, rich in diversity, and which have gradually become impoverished, extinguished, flattened into a dangerous and sterile uniformity? First, it was the turn of the artisans who were no longer able to work in the city center, then the universities and their students, who were confined to specialized areas. Then it was the turn of hospitals, courts, and, finally, residents who were inevitably expelled from city centers so that tourists could stay in their place. Entire cities, rich in culture, art, history, and creative capacities, have been transformed into specialized areas for the enjoyment of tourists. How long can they last before they are lost forever?

A city without biodiversity has no defenses. Think about it: Isn't a high-diversity urban organism so much more alive and resilient? If something goes wrong in a diffuse city, a thousand other activities can immediately make up for the damage, but in a specialized city, when its raison d'être is lacking, what happens? There is no specialization that holds. We saw this during the Covid epidemic: Just two years without tourists was enough and some cities specializing in tourism found themselves on the verge of bankruptcy. Did they learn anything? It doesn't look like it. Will cities organized in this way be able to withstand the coming changes in the environment? What will happen to the economy of these cities when it gets so hot in the summer that the number of tourists inevitably starts to decrease? In fact, we must not make the mistake of forgetting that global warming will drastically change the climate of *all* cities. In this scenario, more diffuse cities, in which most of the needs of citizens can be met without long journeys and in which each district is built in such a way as to guarantee the highest possible biodiversity, are a prerequisite for resistance.

Remember what we said about species: Specialist species have an advantage as long as everything in their niche remains stable, but when the environment is subject to change, then generalist species are by far the most able to resist. So what we need in order to face the coming years with greater security are plant-based, generalist cities, built according to a decentralized and diffuse organization.

Eight

TREEWAYS

The inescapable fact from which to start is that in the coming years global warming will transform our climate and the environment in which we live with a force that we have never experienced in the entire history of human civilization. How to prepare our cities for these changes is the question for which we must find a practical and efficient answer as soon as possible. I believe that the only serious way to prepare for such a diverse and unstable future is to make our cities greener, more permeable, and as diffuse as possible. Especially greener. The main distinction between the cities that will be able to adapt to global warming and those that will suffer its consequences will be the number of trees and vegetation present within them. We need to cover our cities with plants, and we don't have much time to do it. Unfortunately, this is not a small change, and I doubt, frankly, that many cities will be able to make even minimal progress in this direction. In fact, most city dwellers and city administrators have no idea of the magnitude of the climate changes now in progress, and they continue to act as if the problem did not exist, an unwise behavior that will lead many cities to face a decisive crisis without any preparation.

Wanting a different city, covered with trees and vegetation, in direct communication with the surrounding nature, requires not only understanding the scientific reasons for the choice but also overcoming a deep-seated cultural barrier: our idea of the city that, unconsciously or not, we imagine as a place clearly separated from the nature that surrounds it. This is a primitive view, directly linked to the history of our species, an idea that pictures nature as something to be subdued or feared, or, in any case, not as something so important that we cannot live without it.

Step by step, the idea of nature itself has slowly been reposited in the catalog of obsolete ideas, effectively removed from any discussion of our future. We have also removed it from our language, replaced in the contemporary lexicon by the omnipresent *environment*. Respect for the environment has replaced respect for nature, the suffering environment has taken the place of suffering nature. Nature and environment have been treated synonymously, even though, as is evident, they are not the same thing at all.

Yet we are talking about a key concept, a term that was still defined in 1976 as the "most complex word" in our languages.[1] Etymologically, *nature* derives from the Latin *natus*, "to be born," and in Latin it is in turn a translation of the Greek word *physis*, "the fundamental reality, the principle of all things." In Homer, nature is a term associated with the intrinsic characteristics of a plant: "with that the giant killer handed over the magic herb, pulling it from the earth, and Hermes showed me all its name and nature."[2] Plants, once again, are at the origin of everything. Since without plants there could be no animal life, they are the very essence of nature—the nature of nature—the fundamental reality of life on the planet. Nature is the very essence of things, that which makes things what they are and, as such, is independent of human will.

That's why we perceive it as something external to us. Not having the ability to determine its course, like the fox with the grapes, we have decided to ignore it, believing that it has little to do with us. A crazy idea that logically should have disappeared on November 24, 1859, when Charles Darwin, publishing *On the Origin of Species*, clarified once and for all that the human species, having evolved through a slow process of selection, is part of nature, inextricably linked to all other species by a network of relationships whose integrity is necessary for our survival. But science is one thing and our ancient beliefs are another. Thus, in the very same years as Darwin, during the Industrial Revolution, our perception of the essence of nature veered decisively toward something external to man, and the conquest of nature became synonymous with the progress of civilization. In those years, George Perkins Marsh, America's first ecologist and the ambassador to the United Kingdom of Italy from 1861 to 1882, was convinced that man's mission was to subjugate and domesticate nature, because "wherever man fails to master nature, he can but be her slave."[3]

Today, two centuries later, the situation has, if possible, deteriorated even more. Not only do we not feel part of the natural process but we are outside and above it. Nature is all that is wild, untamed. An obstacle to human survival. This is the prevailing idea that we come up against every time we try to think about the city as an area contiguous to nature. For many, cities are the places of humans, not nature. That the two things must remain well separated is a concept so deeply engraved in the history of cities that it seems unshakable. Since the creation of our first settlements, their main function has been to defend us from nature; to protect ourselves from rain, cold, and the danger posed by predators. It has been 12,000 years since the first stirrings of human civilization, but the distrust of nature has remained intact. We would like barren cities in which the only species free to circulate is our own. As in those Renaissance representations of the ideal city in which there is no trace of living beings, we imagine the city as the realization of our naïve idea of reality.

And if you think I'm exaggerating and that in recent years, as a consequence of the climate catastrophe and the unequivocal unsustainability of our cities, this idea has changed radically, consider the furious protests of citizens in the hundreds of cities of Europe that have simply experimented with not cutting the grass in public parks as frequently as they did a few years ago, in order to leave time for some plants to bloom and many insects to frequent them. Leave aside the few shining examples of enlightened cities that, thanks to the stubbornness of their administrators, are starting to do something to make them greener and therefore more resistant. Forget Paris, which, thanks to the unwavering will of its mayor, has surrounded one of its most famous monuments, Notre-Dame cathedral, with a real forest, and try, instead, to ask yourself what usually happens when it is proposed to plant a few trees to reduce heat islands in historic centers. Out of a hundred proposals, ninety-nine are rejected because they are incompatible with the architectural style of the neighborhood and would modify that completely mineral idea of the city. How is it possible to achieve the drastic change that would be needed to resist global warming, when even such ridiculously limited proposals as putting trees along a street are steadfastly opposed? In Florence, a significant part of the city's intelligentsia opposed the project, belittled as a "grammatical error," to plant about fifty saplings along a street of no special architectural value in the historic center. The reason for their opposition was that there have never been trees in the center of Florence. How can we make all these people understand that the threat to our historic centers is not planting trees but rather that not planting them will change the face of our cities forever?

Remedies to make cities more equipped to adapt to the consequences of global warming are available and they would make our cities more resilient and more beautiful, but they require much stronger measures than planting a few trees. To implement these solutions, the majority of the population must be convinced of their fundamental usefulness, something that can only be achieved through education, with a great literacy program about the risks of global warming. A lot of people, most people, have no idea what it is. The gap that exists on this subject, between the knowledge acquired by the scientific community and its diffusion within the population, is dramatically enormous. Uninterrupted sequences of catastrophic events, the probability of which would be insignificant without global warming, are perceived as mere unfortunate coincidences—not part of a larger pattern—and are reported as such by the media. This lack of understanding is not so much a consequence of the low level of education—indeed, it seems that the acceptance of global warming has no correlation with the degree of scientific literacy[4]—but of most people's inability to imagine how an average temperature just 2°C (3.6°F) higher can really change our daily lives. Those who protest because trees would spoil the magnificent profile of the city's architecture do so because they are perfectly capable of imagining what the streets they love would look like with trees, but they are not able to imagine them at temperatures of 2° or 3°C (3.6° to 5.4° F) higher.

We have repeatedly mentioned that the presence of massive tree coverage is one of the key factors for the future of cities. And while I'm sure many readers are well aware of why, it's perhaps worth saying a few words about why trees are so important before we begin to figure out how to plant the millions of trees needed in the fully developed and impermeable areas typical of our urban centers.

The main reason for the importance of trees is easy to explain. They cool the environment, an effect that in a period of global warming is by no means secondary. In fact, to be even more precise, we don't know of anything that is as effective as trees in cooling an urban center.

That a tree, and every plant in proportion to its dimensions, can cool its surrounding environment is due to concurring factors: shading and evapotranspiration. Shading, by reducing the amount of solar radiation that directly or indirectly affects a surface, lowers its temperature, while evapotranspiration cools the environment through the passage of water present in the soil to the vapor state due to the combined effect of transpiration, through the plant, and direct evaporation from the soil. Since the process of evaporation of water is endodermal—that is, it absorbs heat from the environment—the amount of heat absorbed, especially during the summer, can lead to a decrease in air temperature by up to 5° to 6°C (9° to 11°F) compared to treeless areas. If, however, we consider the surface temperatures of buildings or soils, then the differences can reach much higher values, between 8° and 12°C (14.4° and 21.6°F).[5]

Although the cooling effect alone would be enough to make trees our most valuable ally in the fight against global warming, we must always be aware that this is not the only benefit that trees give us. Thanks to trees, we have a) a

reduction in energy consumption due to the cooling of buildings and, therefore, to a lower demand for air-conditioning;
b) improved air quality, because by reducing energy demand,
trees and vegetation decrease the production of associated
air pollution and greenhouse gas emissions, as well as directly removing air pollutants and sequestering carbon dioxide; and, finally, c) they guarantee better management of
rainwater by filtering the water and functioning as buffers
that slow down its entry into the urban drainage system. In
short, without even mentioning the enormous benefits that
trees and vegetation bring to human health and aesthetics,
it should be evident that there is nothing like trees to coun-
teract the consequences of global warming.

The problem is where to put them. In most urban centers, the areas available for planting trees are limited and,
even in the few fortunate cases where these areas exist in
sufficient quantities, they are designated for uses other
than planting trees. Thus, for one reason or another, the
total number of trees that could be planted in cities without
major urban revolutions is often quite insignificant. And indeed, the few hundreds or thousands of trees planted on average each year by a medium-size European city, although
often touted as numbers to be satisfied about, amount to
such a small quantity that their contribution to the cooling of the city is negligible. The number of trees we should
plant in the city is much higher: not thousands of trees but
hundreds of thousands of trees. All the trees that can be
planted and not one less. So, again, where to put them?

Since the readily available surfaces offer the possibility to host only a very small fraction of the trees needed, we must create new space by using areas that have hitherto been used for other purposes. This is simple common sense: If there is no more room, we must identify those areas whose present use is not a priority, and which can easily be converted into places where we can grow trees in the necessary numbers. So if we study cities spread across the entire planet, what are they made up of? Or rather, how is the space that delimits a city distributed?

When looking for details on the distribution of space in cities, it is not easy to find comparable data. Quite intuitively, the surface area of a city should be divided between buildings, streets, and open spaces. However, finding data on how much space on average is occupied by each of the three factors is complex. The proportion of urban land area occupied by streets, for example, can vary greatly from city to city, depending on its history, urbanization, population density, urban design, and many other factors. In general, streets and associated infrastructure can occupy between 20 and 40 percent of the total urban area, up to higher percentages in those cities that have a heavy dependence on cars, as is frequently the case in the United States. In these cases, streets and parking lots account for 35 to 50 percent of the entire urban area.[6]

The same problems arise when looking for data on the area occupied by buildings and open spaces. However, with a little patience and a good dose of approximation, it can be said that the surface of a city is made up of a third streets and associated infrastructure, a third buildings, and a third open spaces.[7] Now, open spaces are those areas (squares, parks, flower beds, sidewalks, riverfronts, beaches, etc.) that are normally already considered when it comes to planting new trees. To be clear, these areas include all those places in the city already covered with trees and where, except in residual cases, it is not possible to imagine planting many others. As for the surfaces on which the buildings stand, except for small interventions on the buildings, such as green roofs and trees on the terraces, the impact of which is minimal, not much else can be done. What's left are streets and associated infrastructure. It all adds up to a quantity of space that in many cities around the world represents a significant share of the urban area and that should be significantly reduced in favor of tree-lined areas.

Meanwhile, what are streets? It seems like a totally idle question, whose answer, however, is not so obvious. Today we perceive streets as places for cars. A space forbidden to people and intended for vehicular traffic only. But if we look, even quickly, at the history of our streets and what they have been used for over time, we realize that this has not always been the case. For centuries, streets were public spaces, frequented by people, places of socialization, play, public representation, markets, where transportation was a tolerated nuisance.

The idea that streets are intended for the exclusive use of vehicles, so much so that they are forbidden to pedestrians, is very recent, dating back only a hundred years. To find out how their use has changed, try looking at a photo from the beginning of the last century that represents the streets of a city you know. The great boulevards, the boulevards of our historic cities, which today are crisscrossed by uninterrupted streams of cars, were places for quiet walks, and most of the squares, later transformed into horrible parking lots, still had the function for which they were built: to be a beautiful place to meet. It is true that back then, as can be seen from photos and films of the time, people walked as they do today mainly on the sidewalks. However, the reason why they did so was entirely different. People walked on the sidewalks not because they were obliged to do so but for the simple fact that they were cleaner and less dusty than the streets.

To explain the prevailing idea at that time, we must consider that in the event of an accident, blaming the driver was totally automatic. The driver could not use excuses such as "the child came out of the blue," because the answer would have been that this is exactly what children normally do. Peter Norton uses an illuminating metaphor to explain the different relationship with the road: It is as if today someone riding a motorcycle in the hallway of a house collided with a person. The biker couldn't defend himself with "Oh, well, they jumped out at me," because, of course, no one expects anyone to ride something as dangerous as a motorcycle in a hallway. Until the early 1920s, the streets were still like the hallways of our homes.[8]

It was during this period that, in the United States, the first misunderstandings began to arise about who had or did not have the right to use city streets. In the cradle of Fordism, in urban contexts where there was no restriction on passage on the roads, neither for cars nor for people, for the first time the ratio of one car for every ten inhabitants was exceeded (today the ratio is one for every inhabitant)— a ratio that, just to make a comparison, was reached in Italy only in the early 1960s—and this caused an enormous number of fatal accidents (especially considered in relation to the low number of cars). In the four years after the end of World War I, more people died in automobile accidents in the United States than had died during the entire war; in the 1920s there were more than 200,000 victims, most of them children playing in the streets of the city.[9] This staggering number of deaths was the direct consequence of the arrival of cars on the streets, which continued to be perceived by everyone as a space belonging to pedestrians.

Then things changed quickly. City administrations began to adopt simple rules on the coexistence between people and cars and imposed ever lower speed limits on cars. Until the citizens of some cities, such as Cincinnati, Ohio, alarmed about the increasing number of fatal accidents, voted to have a referendum that, if they had won, would have required every motorist to have a mechanical speed limiter directly connected to the car's power supply, which would limit the vehicle's speed to below 24 miles per hour. The straightforward equation of speed and danger to people led the powerful American automobile industry to take a firm stand on the referendum, comparing it to a return to the Stone Age, and to deploy all its power to change once and for all the prevailing concept of road use. If the idea that speed was a problem had been accepted, the car industry would have lost its main selling point: that thanks to cars it was possible to move faster than by any other means. A fundamental advantage for an animal that makes the speed of getting away its best answer to any problem.

The auto industry came up with a campaign to reframe all the arguments about road safety, reversing the attribution of blame. Accidents occurred not because the vehicles were dangerous but because pedestrians, heedless of the vehicles, behaved recklessly by walking down streets without paying attention. This is where the reversal of roles and the ceding of the sovereignty of our streets to cars began. The technique with which the car companies facilitated this reversal of roles was a small masterpiece of manipulation. On the one hand, the strategy called for cities to issue a series of regulations as soon as possible, so that pedestrians could no longer walk along the roadbed but were required to stay on the sidewalks and cross the street only at crosswalks.

At the same time, a more subtle operation was carried out in concert with the local police and various groups, such as the Boy Scouts. Its goal was to shame, if not ostracize people who still walked in the streets. An important part of this strategy was the adoption of the term *jaywalker*, a new word that described those who still walked the streets

Until the advent of car traffic, streets were not considered a place where pedestrians were prohibited. The boulevards of our cities were places of quiet walks, as shown by this photo of Sixth Avenue in New York taken at the beginning of the twentieth century. Most people are walking on the sidewalk because it is cleaner, but many are walking undisturbed along the street.

unaware of the refined rules and necessities of city life. In short, a hick, a rube. From that moment on, thanks to special laws that regulated the behavior of pedestrians, the streets no longer belonged to people but to cars. In Europe, the process was more or less the same, only slightly shifted in time, with some differences because most European cities, having a longer history, also have a very different structure from American cities. In Italy, for example, the advent of car traffic meant not only the disappearance of the streets as public places but also the even more painful disappearance of many historic piazzas that became huge parking lots in the middle of cities. Even in Hawaii, the advent of cars and parking lots often spoiled what had been the landscape of a tropical paradise, a turn of events that inspired Joni Mitchell to write her song "Big Yellow Taxi," where paradise is paved to put up a parking lot and all the trees are put in a tree museum.[10]

Today, these disgraceful eyesores have (almost) completely disappeared. It's hard to find a historic piazza that still serves as a parking lot. Think about what a revolution the reappropriation of such important spaces has been. Only a few years have passed since most of our historic centers and piazzas were buried under mountains of cars, and yet, when we look at those images, they seem to date back to a much more remote and barbaric period. That's a good sign; today no one, except for a few deranged people, would ever think of transforming historic piazzas into open-air parking lots. In the same way, I am convinced that, within a few years, we will look with disgust at the images of our streets covered with parked or moving cars. In this near future, streets returned to their rightful owners will be covered with trees that will perform the invaluable tasks of lowering the temperature, permitting nature to permeate urban centers, and allowing people to enjoy a newfound community with other living beings.

Do you think this is impossible? That we will never be able to give up car traffic on our streets and that, in any case, the disadvantages of such a choice would be far greater than the benefits? I do not agree. Closing a good percentage of our streets to traffic for good and turning them into city forests is not at all impossible. Just as it was not impossible to close our historic centers to traffic or remove parked cars from our piazzas. At first the problems seem insurmountable, but in a short time the advantages become so obvious as to render the small (if any) inconveniences they entail irrelevant.

When it comes to changing our cities for the better, the story of Curitiba is truly one of the most brilliant examples that can be cited.[11] Curitiba is a city in the south of Brazil, in the state of Paraná, which today has around two million inhabitants.

Today it would not be tolerable to imagine one of our historic piazzas disfigured by the presence of thousands of cars. Yet, until not so many years ago, the most beautiful squares of our cities were used as open-air parking lots, as seen in this 1960s photo of Piazza Plebiscito in Naples.

In 1971, a young architect named Jaime Lerner was elected mayor of Curitiba. He found himself governing a city with an urgent need to manage its tumultuous population growth. In 1972, the transformation that Lerner had envisioned for his city began with the streets. Or rather, with a single street, now known as Rua das Flores, which was, literally overnight, closed to traffic and made the first pedestrian island in Brazil.

Lerner, perfectly aware of the fierce opposition that such an idea would arouse, was looking for a way to prevent the project from being blocked. So on a Friday evening, after the courthouse had closed and no one could stop him, he invaded the center of the city at the head of a group of workers and began planting trees, arranging planters, depaving roads, installing lamps, and erecting benches in what until the day before had been one of the busiest streets in the city. The teams of workers alternated, without interruption, until Monday morning, when, before the reopening of the courthouse, pedestrianization had become a reality, making Rua das Flores the first pedestrian island in Brazil and, at the same time, the fastest public work ever built in the country.

Of course, it wasn't that simple, and the disgruntled citizens, among whom the merchants were undoubtedly the most active, tried in every way to make Lerner retrace his steps. To no avail. Whenever someone tried to damage the project, the workers of the municipality came to restore it. If gangs of boys uprooted the plants, teams of gardeners would promptly replace them. If the barriers were vandalized, operators would repair them. If the benches were removed, someone would put them back in place.

In many of his interviews, Lerner said that his goal was to hold out for six months. He was certain that after that long the citizenry would realize the enormous number of advantages and would no longer protest. That's exactly what happened: The merchants realized that their businesses were doing better than before, and they not only stopped protesting but demanded that pedestrianization be extended to other areas of the city. The same thing happened for the other citizens who suddenly found themselves frequenting streets where it was now possible to walk.

Lerner continued to administer Curitiba (he was mayor for three terms), implementing an innovative bus rapid transit system that is imitated today by hundreds of other cities in the world, and above all creating dozens of parks and planting millions of trees in the city, so as to increase the amount of public green space from just under 1 square meter (10.7 square feet) to 55 square meters (592 square feet) per person in just a few years. Today, it is no coincidence that Curitiba is one of the most exemplary cities in Brazil with high rates of education and tourism.

Jane Jacobs, an anthropologist and urban development theorist, has written: "Think of a city and what comes to mind? Its streets. If a city's streets look interesting, the city looks interesting; if they look dull, the city looks dull."[12] Every road occupied by cars loses its character: It is not only boring but ugly and, worse, it is useless and harmful. Useless because in a well-organized city, there would be little or no need for private cars, and harmful because a good share of greenhouse gases, as well as numerous other pollutants that cause global warming, are directly linked to urban transportation.

By drastically reducing the surface area of the city dedicated to car traffic and using this reclaimed space to plant trees and create parks, we would achieve the double result of reducing emissions of climate-altering gases (especially carbon dioxide) produced by traffic and increasing the amount of carbon dioxide fixed by trees. In short, with a single operation we would act directly on the causes of global warming and defend ourselves from its consequences, through the cooling action of trees. All in all, a simple solution, which in the beginning would certainly entail small inconveniences and adjustments in the lifestyles of citizens, but which before long, as has happened for the people of Curitiba and for every pedestrianization ever implemented since then, would amply repay any sacrifices. Try to imagine some of the great multilane boulevards, or some of the streets of any order and degree of your cities, transformed into veritable rivers of trees and plants. At first glance they might resemble lush parks in which to walk or cycle around the city, but they would not be parks at all, they would still remain streets, with the shops, services, bars, and residences that overlook them. Only they would be much more beautiful streets. Streets that neither Jacobs nor anyone else could judge to be boring. Above all, they would be city streets preparing to resist the threats of global warming.

There is a city in Brazil, Porto Alegre, where there is a street that could help us imagine what we are talking about. It is called Rua Gonçalo de Carvalho and is often cited as one of the most charming streets on the planet. In the opinion of the justifiably proud citizens of Porto Alegre it is the street *mais bonita do mundo*. There is only one reason for its charm: the trees that grow along its sides and create a sort of dense forest, which creeps right into the center of the city. Imagine a Rua Gonçalo de Carvalho, but without cars; a river of plants that enters our cities using the streets, without separation from the outside. Think about how cities would change, definitively and for the better. I repeat, I see no alternative: It must be done. And the sooner the better.

Have you ever heard of Robert Moses? Chances are this name doesn't mean much to most people. He was an extremely powerful urban planner who, in the middle of the twentieth century, redesigned New York City. His urban planning choices were so important that many have compared his work to that of Baron Haussmann in Paris. Moses saw the car as the supreme symbol of progress and modernity. Like many Americans, he perceived the automobile as a necessary tool to guarantee the freedom of the individual. Though he knew full well that to build the hundreds of miles of roads needed to implement his vision, neighborhoods would have to be torn down, often displacing entire communities, this was not something that disturbed him excessively. Automobiles were the most powerful tool of American progress, so it followed that cities had to be built to facilitate this progress, not to slow it down. Following this questionable urban planning thesis even at a time when the environmental problem did not yet exist, Moses and many others like him multiplied in a few years the number and width of roads and streets in American cities. Theirs was an energetic and large-scale undertaking that changed the face of cities in the United States and, subsequently, of many other cities on the planet. Between the 1960s and 1970s, the number of large roads carrying traffic in and out of cities grew rapidly. Moses is credited with a famous phrase that I think has great relevance to the current discussion about the future of cities. To justify his nonchalant approach to the use of backhoes and bulldozers in urban centers, he apparently used to say, "You can't make an omelet without breaking some eggs." If it was necessary to ensure a smooth passage for automobiles, it could not be done without demolishing neighborhoods, destroying forests, and asphalting soil.

Well, today eggs must be broken to make a different omelet. Just as in a few years, driven by the need for progress and above all by the powerful motor vehicle industry (let's not forget that), the face of cities was disfigured by the creation of new roads, today with no less efficiency, in light of the changed conditions brought about by global warming, we must act by closing those same roads to traffic and turning them into *treeways*. Every city that has the good of its citizens at heart should act in this direction and without delay. Any small inconveniences, certainly not comparable to the gutting of entire neighborhoods, will have to be treated with the same philosophy as Moses's omelet.

But what are these inconveniences we are talking about? How could the creation of treeways limit our freedom, or even our ability to progress? The main objection is, of course, related to travel: If we close streets and roads, how will we get around in the city? Sure, but the idea is not to close all streets to vehicular traffic; a good part of them, yes, but not all of them. In addition, on the treeways you could move on foot or by bicycle, which is the best way—for those who can—to get around the city, and of course there should be an excellent public transportation network.

We must always keep in mind that in cities, space is a resource to be used as efficiently as possible to meet the needs of the inhabitants. Today, there is a significant difference in the space required by the different modes of transportation. Active modes, such as walking or cycling, are up to twenty times more space-efficient than using a medium-size car. Car-based systems also require infrastructure such as roads and parking lots, which must be quantified in the amount of space consumed. Just think of the huge amount of space reserved for car parking. In some American cities such as Las Vegas, more than 30 percent of the city's surface area is allocated to parking, but even in the densest European cities this percentage continues to be high. Except for a few urban centers that have been moving for years to reduce the number of available parking spaces (an example is London), in the remaining cases the goal has always been the opposite: to increase the surface area allocated to parking not only to accommodate the growing number of vehicles but also to adapt parking spaces to the growing size of cars—a madness that few seem to worry about. The size of cars in Europe for the best-selling models has increased dramatically in recent years, partly for safety reasons, partly to accommodate a taller population, and partly because the market demands larger and larger models. In Great Britain, the top five best-selling models in 1965 had an average width of 1.5 meters (5 feet) and a length of 3.9 meters (12 feet, 9 inches). In 2020, again for the five best-selling models, the dimensions had increased to 1.8 meters (5 feet, 11 inches) wide and 4.3 meters (14 feet) long. If you do two simple surface calculations by approximating the shape of a car to a rectangle, you will see that this is a 32 percent increase in the area occupied by cars. Larger dimensions mean taking up an extra chunk of road when the car is in motion and having to provide additional space in the parking lots for vehicle access and entry and exit maneuvers. Cars, therefore, need a lot of surface area. A quantity of space that, when compared to other forms of transportation, becomes difficult to justify.

To get a clearer picture of what we are talking about, the concept of the *spatial footprint* of transportation is useful, an indicator in square meters or square feet of the area allocated to transportation in the city. The resulting figure can be assigned to an entire category of transportation (space intended for buses or cars or bicycles) or to an individual citizen using one of these vehicles. Without going into technicalities, it is certain that a pedestrian or a bicycle will need much less space, both during the journey and when stopped, than a car. In the same way, considering the large number of people transported, public transportation has a much smaller spatial footprint than private cars.

A city that wants to transform a significant portion of its streets into treeways could easily do so by increasing the efficiency of public transportation, encouraging active means of transportation (walking and cycling), and discouraging, in every way possible, automobile traffic. Every car that is no longer used frees up a lot of space in the city (including roads, infrastructure, and parking lots) in which, much more effectively for the health of city dwellers and their environment, a tree could be planted.

I know that at this point many of you are thinking that, yes, it would be nice, but it is impossible to imagine closing roads and streets. Or that perhaps it could be done, but first we would have to improve the condition and efficiency of public transportation. That without some alternative form of mobility it is unthinkable, etc. Not to mention the "more-than-that-ers" or the ones who say, "If only all we had to do was cover the streets with trees, but our cities' problems are so much more than that." I say, simply: Let's do it. We must act as Lerner did in Curitiba, overnight, from one day to the next. And stick to our guns until the benefits become apparent even to the hardest of heads and hearts. Let's turn our streets into treeways without waiting for every other piece of the puzzle to fall into place. I have great faith in the ability of our species to self-organize. If a street is closed to traffic, people will find the most efficient alternatives on their own. It's not necessary that city administrations adjust everything down to the last detail. Their main function today is to make our cities resistant to global warming, and covering them with trees is one of the few wise things that can be done.

NOTES

1. MAN IS THE MEASURE OF ALL THINGS

1. Sheena S. Iyengar and Mark R. Lepper, "When Choice Is Demotivating: Can One Desire Too Much of a Good Thing?," *Journal of Personality and Social Psychology* 79, no. 6 (2000): 995–1006.
2. Yinon M. Bar-On, Rob Phillips, and Ron Milo, "The Biomass Distribution on Earth," *Proceedings of the National Academy of Sciences of the United States of America* 115, no. 25 (2018): 6506–11.
3. Martin-Brehm Christensen et al., *Survival of the Richest: How We Must Tax the Super-rich Now to Fight Inequality* (Oxford: Oxfam International, 2023).
4. Stefano Mancuso, *Planting Our World*, translated by Gregory Conti (New York: Other Press, 2020).
5. Duane Isely, *One Hundred and One Botanists* (Ames, IA: Iowa State University Press, 1994), 184.
6. Giovanni Aloi, *Lucian Freud Herbarium* (München-London-New York: Prestel, 2019).
7. André Félibien, *Conférences de l'académie royale de peinture et de sculpture pendant l'année 1667* (Paris: Léonard, 1668), preface.
8. Lawrence Gowing, *Lucian Freud* (London: Thames & Hudson, 1982).

2. THE BODY BECOMES ARCHITECTURE

1. William Morris, *Prospects of Architecture in Civilization* (1881).
2. Rudolf Wittkower, *Architectural Principles in the Age of Humanism* (Originally published as vol. 19 of the Studies of the Warburg Institute). London: University of London Press, 1949.
3. Marco Vitruvio Pollione, *De architectura* (Pordenone: Edizioni Studio Tesi, 1990), 162–63.
4. Le Corbusier, *Le modulor. Essai sur une mesure harmonique à l'échelle humaine applicable universellement à l'architecture et à la mécanique* (Boulogne: Éditions de l'Architecture d'Aujourd'hui, 1950).
5. Ibid.
6. James Crabtree, "Le Corbusier's Chandigarh: An Indian City Unlike Any Other," *Financial Times*, July 3, 2015.
7. Peter Hall, *Cities of Tomorrow: An Intellectual History of Urban Planning and Design Since 1880* (Chichester: Wiley Blackwell, 2014), 246.
8. Le Corbusier, *My Work* (London: The Architectural Press, 1960), 155.

3. THE EVOLVING CITY

1. Charles Darwin, *The Autobiography of Charles Darwin (1809–1882): With Original Omissions Restored* (1958), 106, available at http://darwin-online.org.uk/content/frameset?itemID=F1497&viewtype=text&pageseq=1.
2. Patrick Geddes, *Cities in Evolution: An Introduction to the Town Planning Movement and to the Study of Cities* (London: Williams & Norgate, 1915), 26.
3. Cited in "Biology of Cities," *Time*, November 30, 1942.
4. Thomas Hobbes, *Leviathan: Or the Matter, Forme and Power of a Commonwealth, Ecclesiastical and Civil*, edited by Michael Oakeshott (New York: Simon and Shuster, 1962), 101.
5. Thomas Huxley, "The Struggle for Existence in Human Society (1888)," in *Evolution and Ethics, and Other Essays* (London: Macmillan & Co., 1894), 195–236, quote is on 204.

6. Siân Reynolds, "French Connections: The Scientific, Academic and Political Networks of Patrick Geddes in France (1870s–1900)," in *Liens personnels, réseaux, solidarités en France et dans les îles Britanniques (xie-xxe siècle)*, edited by David Bates and Véronique Gazeau (Paris: Éditions de la Sorbonne, 2006).

7. Élisée Reclus, "Pages de sociologie préhistorique," *L'Humanité Nouvelle* (February 1898): 129–43, quote is on 138.

8. Léon Metchnikoff, preface, in Élisée Reclus, *La civilisation et les grands fleuves historiques* (Paris: Hachette, 1889), xxvii–xxviii.

9. Lynn Margulis, "Symbiosis and Evolution," *Scientific American* 225, no. 2 (1971): 48–57.

10. Pëtr A. Kropotkin, *Mutual Aid: A Factor of Evolution* (New York: McClure Phillips & Co., 1902), vii.

4. THE SURVIVAL OF THE FITTEST

1. Arthur G. Tansley, "The Use and Abuse of Vegetational Concepts and Terms," *Ecology* 16, no. 3 (1935): 284–307.

2. Ibid.

3. H. Bernard D. Kettlewell, "Selection Experiments on Industrial Melanism in the *Lepidoptera*," *Heredity* 9 (1955): 323–42.

4. Noah M. Reid et al., "The Genomic Landscape of Rapid Repeated Evolutionary Adaptation to Toxic Pollution in Wild Fish," *Science* 354, no. 6317 (2016): 1305–08.

5. Katharine Byrne and Richard A. Nichols, "*Culex pipiens* in London Underground Tunnels: Differentiation Between Surface and Subterranean Populations," *Heredity* 82 (1999): 7–15.

6. Menno Schilthuizen, *Darwin Comes to Town: How the Urban Jungle Drives Evolution* (London: Quercus, 2018).

7. Kristien I. Brans and Luc De Meester, "City Life on Fast Lanes: Urbanization Induces an Evolutionary Shift Towards a Faster Lifestyle in the Water Flea *Daphnia*," *Functional Ecology* 32, no. 9 (2018): 2225–40.

8. Kristien I. Brans et al., "The Heat Is On: Genetic Adaptation to Urbanization Mediated by Thermal Tolerance and Body Size," *Global Change Biology* 23 (2017): 5218–27.

9. Sangeet Lamichhaney et al., "Evolution of Darwin's Finches and Their Beaks Revealed by Genome Sequencing," *Nature* 518 (2015): 371–75.

10. Charles Darwin, *On the Origin of Species* (London: The Folio Society, 2006), 315–16.

11. Matthew Combs et al., "Spatial Population Genomics of the Brown Rat (*Rattus norvegicus*) in New York City," *Molecular Ecology* 27, no. 1 (2018): 83–98.

12. Matthew Combs et al., "Urban Rat Races: Spatial Population Genomics of Brown Rats (*Rattus norvegicus*) Compared Across Multiple Cities," *Proceedings of the Royal Society B* 285 (2018): 20180245.

13. Pierre-Olivier Cheptou et al., "Rapid Evolution of Seed Dispersal in an Urban Environment in the Weed *Crepis sancta*," *Proceedings of the National Academy of Sciences of the United States of America* 105, no. 10 (2008): 3796–99.

14. Marc T. J. Johnson and Jason Munshi-South, "Evolution of Life in Urban Environments," *Science* 358, no. 6363 (2017): eaam8327.

15. Ernst Mayr, "Change of Genetic Environment and Evolution," in *Evolution as a Process*, edited by Julian Huxley, A. C. Hardy, and E. B. Ford (London: Allen & Unwin, 1954), 157–80.

16. Edmond Bordage, "Le repeuplement végétal et animal des îles Krakatoa depuis l'éruption de 1883," *Annales de Géographie* 133 (1916): 1–22.

17. Stefano Mancuso, *The Incredible Journey of Plants* (New York: Other Press, 2020).

18. Mae K. A. Johnson et al., "The Role of Spines in Anthropogenic Seed Dispersal on the Galápagos Islands," *Ecology and Evolution* 10, no. 3 (2020): 1639–47.

19. L. Ruth Rivkin et al., "Urbanization Alters Interactions Between Darwin's Finches and *Tribulus cistoides* on the Galápagos Islands," *Ecology and Evolution* 11, no. 22 (2021): 15754–65.

20. United Nations, *World Urbanization Prospects 2018* (New York: United Nations, 2019).

21. This data is from the Gridded Population of the World and Global Rural-Urban Mapping Project, Socioeconomic Data and Applications Center, Columbia University, New York.

22. Kees Klein Goldewijk, Arthur Beusen, and Peter Janssen, "Long-term Dynamic Modeling of Global Population and Built-up Area in a Spatially Explicit Way: HYDE 3.1," *The Holocene* 20, no. 4 (2010): 565–73.

23. Debbie Guatelli-Steinberg, *What Teeth Reveal About Human Evolution* (Cambridge and New York: Cambridge University Press, 2016).

24. George H. Perry et al., "Diet and the Evolution of Human Amylase Gene Copy Number Variation," *Nature Genetics* 39 (2007): 1256–60.

25. Richard P. Evershed et al., "Dairying, Diseases and the Evolution of Lactase Persistence in Europe," *Nature* 608 (2022): 336–45.

26. Todd Bersaglieri et al., "Genetic Signatures of Strong Recent Positive Selection at the Lactase Gene," *The American Journal of Human Genetics* 74, no. 6 (2004): 1111–20.

27. Gebhard Flatz and Hans W. Rotthauwe, "Lactose Nutrition and Natural Selection," *The Lancet* 302, no. 7820 (1973): 76–77.

28. Peter Deplazes et al., "Wilderness in the City: The Urbanization of *Echinococcus multilocularis*," *Trends in Parasitology* 20, no. 2 (2004): 77–84.

29. Amber N. Wright and Matthew E. Gompper, "Altered Parasite Assemblages in Raccoons in Response to Manipulated Resource Availability," *Oecologia* 144, no. 1 (2005): 148–56.

30. Albert Camus, *The Plague* (London: Hamish Hamilton,1948).

31. Tom Paulson, "Epidemiology: A Mortal Foe," *Nature* 502, no. 7470 (2013): S2–S3.

32. World Health Organization, *Global Tuberculosis Report 2022* (Geneva: WHO, 2022).

33. Ian Barnes et al., "Ancient Urbanization Predicts Genetic Resistance to Tuberculosis," *Evolution* 65, no. 3 (2011): 842–48.
34. Richard Fuller et al., "Pollution and Health: A Progress Update," *The Lancet Planetary Health* 6, no. 6 (2022): e535–47.
35. Karn Vohra et al., "Global Mortality from Outdoor Fine Particle Pollution Generated by Fossil Fuel Combustion: Results from GEOS-Chem," *Environmental Research* 195 (2021): 110754.
36. Alan Macfarlane, *The Savage Wars of Peace: England, Japan and the Malthusian Trap* (Oxford: Blackwell, 1997).
37. Fuller et al., "Pollution and Health."

5. URBAN METABOLISM

1. Patrick Geddes, "An Analysis of the Principles of Economics," *Proceedings of the Royal Society of Edinburgh* 12, no. 113 (1885): 943–80.
2. Mathis Wackernagel and William E. Rees, *Our Ecological Footprint: Reducing Human Impact on the Earth* (Gabriola Island, BC: New Society Publishers, 1996), 9.
3. Wafaa Baabou et al., "The Ecological Footprint of Mediterranean Cities: Awareness Creation and Policy Implications," *Environmental Science & Policy* 69 (2017): 94–104.
4. Joseph Poore and Thomas Nemecek, "Reducing Food's Environmental Impacts Through Producers and Consumers," *Science* 360, no. 6392 (2018): 987–92.
5. Erle C. Ellis et al., "Anthropogenic Transformation of the Biomes, 1700 to 2000," *Global Ecology and Biogeography* 19, no. 5 (2010): 589–606.
6. Food and Agriculture Organization of the United Nations, *The State of the World's Forests 2022* (Rome: FAO, 2022).
7. Karl Marx, *Das Kapital* (Moscow: Progress Publishers, 1887), vol. 1.
8. Ibid., vol. 3.
9. Jacob Moleschott, *Der Kreislauf des Lebens* (1852), 40, cited in Alfred Schmidt, *Il concetto di natura in Marx* (Bari: Laterza, 1969), 80.

10. Marina Fischer-Kowalski and Helmut Haberl, "Sustainable Development: Socio-economic Metabolism and Colonization of Nature," *International Social Science Journal* 50, no. 158 (1998): 573–87.

11. Abel Wolman, "The Metabolism of Cities," *Scientific American* 213, no. 3 (1965): 178–93.

12. Herbert Girardet, *The Gaia Atlas of Cities* (London: Gaia Books, 1996).

13. David Wachsmuth, "Three Ecologies: Urban Metabolism and the Society-Nature Opposition," *The Sociological Quarterly* 53 (2012): 506–23, quote is on 514.

14. William R. Burnside et al., "Human Macroecology: Linking Pattern and Process in Big-picture Human Ecology," *Biological Reviews* 87, no. 1 (2012): 194–208.

15. Robert Walker et al., "Growth Rates and Life Histories in Twenty-two Small-scale Societies," *American Journal of Human Biology* 18, no. 3 (2006): 295–311.

16. Fridolin Krausmann et al., "The Global Sociometabolic Transition: Past and Present Metabolic Profiles and Their Future Trajectories," *Journal of Industrial Ecology* 12, nos. 5–6 (2008): 637–56.

17. Yadvinder Malhi, "The Metabolism of a Human-dominated Planet," in *Is the Planet Full?*, edited by Ian Goldin (Oxford: Oxford University Press, 2014), 142–63.

18. Geoffrey West, *Scale: The Universal Laws of Growth, Innovation, Sustainability, and the Pace of Life in Organisms, Cities, Economies, and Companies* (London: Penguin, 2017).

19. Edward O. Wilson, *The Social Conquest of Earth* (New York: Liveright, 2012).

20. Luís M. A. Bettencourt et al., "Growth, Innovation, Scaling, and the Pace of Life in Cities," *Proceedings of the National Academy of Sciences of the United States of America* 104, no. 17 (2007): 7301–06.

21. Luís M. A. Bettencourt, "The Origin of Scaling in Cities," *Science* 340, no. 6139 (2013): 1438–41.

6. THE DIFFUSE CITY

1. Ting Wei, Junliang Wu, and Shaoqing Chen, "Keeping Track of Greenhouse Gas Emission Reduction Progress and Targets in 167 Cities Worldwide," *Frontiers in Sustainable Cities* 3 (2021): 696381.

2. Tom K. R. Matthews, Robert L. Wilby, and Conor Murphy, "Communicating the Deadly Consequences of Global Warming for Human Heat Stress," *Proceedings of the National Academy of Sciences of the United States of America* 114, no. 15 (2017): 3861–66.

3. Patrick E. Phelan et al., "Urban Heat Island: Mechanisms, Implications, and Possible Remedies," *Annual Review of Environment and Resources* 40 (2015): 285–307.

4. Tim R. Oke, "The Energetic Basis of the Urban Heat Island," *Quarterly Journal of the Royal Meteorological Society* 108, no. 455 (1982): 1–24.

5. Urban Climate Change Research Network et al., "The Future We Don't Want: How Climate Change Could Impact the World's Greatest Cities," C40 Knowledge Technical Report, February 2018.

6. Available at https://hooge104.shinyapps.io/future_cities_app/.

7. Jean-François Bastin et al., "Understanding Climate Change from a Global Analysis of City Analogues," *PLOS One* 14, no. 7 (2019): e0217592.

8. Matthew C. Fitzpatrick and Robert R. Dunn, "Contemporary Climatic Analogs for 540 North American Urban Areas in the Late 21st Century," *Nature Communications* 10 (2019): 614.

9. Elvira S. Poloczanska et al., "Global Imprint of Climate Change on Marine Life," *Nature Climate Change* 3 (2013): 919–25.

10. Colin J. Carlson et al., "Rapid Range Shifts in African Anopheles Mosquitoes over the Last Century," *Biology Letters* 19, no. 2 (2023): 20220365.

11. Camila González et al., "Climate Change and Risk of Leishmaniasis in North America: Predictions from Ecological Niche Models of Vector and Reservoir Species," *PLOS Neglected Tropical Diseases* 4, no. 1 (2010): e585.

12. Gretta T. Pecl et al., "Biodiversity Redistribution Under Climate Change: Impacts on Ecosystems and Human Well-being," *Science* 355, no. 6332 (2017): eaai9214.

13. Josep Peñuelas et al., "Migration, Invasion and Decline: Changes in Recruitment and Forest Structure in a Warming-linked Shift in European Beech Forest in Catalonia (NE Spain)," *Ecography* 30, no. 6 (2007): 829–37.

14. Leif Kullman, "Rapid Recent Range-margin Rise of Tree and Shrub Species in the Swedish Scandes," *Journal of Ecology* 90, no. 1 (2002): 68–77.

15. Grant P. Elliott, "Treeline Ecotones," in *The International Encyclopedia of Geography*, edited by Douglas Richardson et al. (Chichester: John Wiley & Sons, 2017), 1–10.

16. Xinyue He et al., "Global Distribution and Climatic Controls of Natural Mountain Treelines," *Global Change Biology* (July 2023): 10.1111/gcb.16885.

17. Alan Buis, "Too Hot to Handle: How Climate Change May Make Some Places Too Hot to Live," NASA Jet Propulsion Laboratory, March 9, 2022.

18. Chi Xu et al., "Future of the Human Climate Niche," *Proceedings of the National Academy of Sciences of the United States of America* 117, no. 21 (2020): 11350–55.

19. Colin Raymond et al., "The Emergence of Heat and Humidity Too Severe for Human Tolerance," *Science Advances* 6, no. 19 (2020): eaaw1838.

20. Daniel J. Vecellio et al., "Evaluating the 35°C Wet-bulb Temperature Adaptability Threshold for Young, Healthy Subjects (PSU HEAT Project)," *Journal of Applied Physiology* 132, no. 2 (2022): 340–45.

8. TREEWAYS

1. Raymond Williams, *Keywords: A Vocabulary of Culture and Society* (New York: Oxford University Press, 1985), 164.

2. Homer, *The Odyssey*, translated by Robert Fagles (New York: Penguin, 1996), 240–41.

3. George Perkins Marsh, "The Study of Nature," *Christian Examiner* 68 (1860): 33–62, 24.
4. Lisa Zaval and James F. M. Cornwell, "Effective Education and Communication Strategies to Promote Environmental Engagement," *European Journal of Education* 52, no. 4 (2017): 477–86.
5. Jonas Schwaab et al., "The Role of Urban Trees in Reducing Land Surface Temperatures in European Cities," *Nature Communications* 12 (2021): 6763.
6. Jean-Paul Rodrigue, *The Geography of Transport Systems* (New York: Routledge, 2020).
7. United Nations Human Settlements Programme, *Envisaging the Future of Cities*, World Cities Report 2022, available at https://unhabitat.org/sites/default/files/2022/06/wcr_2022.pdf.
8. Peter Norton, *Fighting Traffic: The Dawn of the Motor Age in the American City*, quoted in Hunter Oatman-Stanford, "Murder Machines: Why Cars Will Kill 30,000 Americans This Year," *Collectors Weekly*, March 10, 2014.
9. Ibid.
10. Joni Mitchell, "Big Yellow Taxi," available at https://en.wikipedia.org/wiki/Big_Yellow_Taxi.
11. Naiara Galarraga Gortázar, "Curitiba: Brazil's Sustainable Green Gem," *El País*, July 2, 2023.
12. Jane Jacobs, *The Death and Life of Great American Cities* (New York: Vintage Books, 1961), 29.

ILLUSTRATION CREDITS

15 H.S. Photos / Alamy Stock Photo.

26 © F.L.C. / ADAGP, Paris / Artists Rights Society (ARS), New York (2024).

28 © F.L.C. / ADAGP, Paris / Artists Rights Society (ARS), New York (2024).

34 The Picture Art Collection / Alamy Stock Photo.

35 Pictorial Press Ltd / Alamy Stock Photo.

36 Historic Images / Alamy Stock Photo.

47 From Charles Darwin, *The Variation of Animals and Plants Under Domestication* (New York: D. Appleton and Company, 1884), vol. 1: 144, 147, 152, 154, 157, 160.

52 Aldona Griskeviciene / Alamy Stock Photo.

55 Library Book Collection / Alamy Stock Photo.

56 Penta Springs Limited / Alamy Stock Photo.

60 Image from Richard Bradley, *A Philosophical Account of the Works of Nature* (London: Mears, 1721), table xxv.

62 Classic Image / Alamy Stock Photo.

69 Image from Jonathan Dubois and Pierre-Olivier Cheptou, "Competition/Colonization Syndrome Mediated by Early Germination in Non-dispersing Achenes in the Heteromorphic Species *Crepis sancta*," *Annals of Botany* 110, no. 6 (2012): 1245–51.

76 Peacock Graphics / Alamy Stock Photo.

102 World History Archive / Alamy Stock Photo.

132 Image from Alexander K. Johnston, *The Physical Atlas: A Series of Maps & Notes Illustrating the Geographical Distribution of Natural Phenomena*, (Edinburgh-London: William Blackwood & Sons, 1848).

135 1 and 2. The Glacier Photograph Collection, National Snow and Ice Data Center.

139 Graphic re-creation from Chi Xu et al., "Future of the Human Climate Niche," *Proceedings of the National Academy of Sciences of the United States of America* 117, no. 21 (2020): 11350–55.

145 Luca Sgualdini / Getty Images.

172 Niday Picture Library / Alamy Stock Photo.

174 The History Collection / Alamy Stock Photo.

ABOUT THE AUTHOR

Stefano Mancuso is one of the world's leading authorities in the field of plant neurobiology, which explores signaling and communication at all levels of biological organization. He is a professor at the University of Florence and has published more than 250 scientific papers in international journals. His previous books include *Planting Our World* (Other Press, 2023), *The Nation of Plants* (Other Press, 2021), *The Incredible Journey of Plants* (Other Press, 2020), *The Revolutionary Genius of Plants: A New Understanding of Plant Intelligence and Behavior*, and *Brilliant Green: The Surprising History and Science of Plant Intelligence*.

ABOUT THE TRANSLATOR

Gregory Conti has translated numerous works of fiction, non-fiction, and poetry from Italian including works by Emilio Lussu, Rosetta Loy, Elisa Biagini, and Paolo Rumiz. He is a regular contributor to the literary quarterly *Raritan*.